The  and The ...ypse

By Cliff Kincaid

Acknowledgements

This book is for the purpose of understanding and overcoming the Marxist rhetoric of dialectical change and the apocalypse America's enemies have planned for us. *The Sword of Revolution and The Communist Apocalypse* is published by America's Survival, Inc. and is made possible by the late Dick Scaife and the Sarah Scaife and Allegheny Foundations. We also want to thank a former intelligence community official, who has chosen to remain anonymous, for his contributions to this book. Oleg Atbashian, a writer and graphic artist from the former USSR, deserves thanks and recognition for another eye-catching book cover. Oleg uses one of Ronald Reagan's favorite weapons -- humor -- to make fun of Marxists and other enemies of America on his website www.thepeoplescube.com

America's Survival, Inc.
Cliff Kincaid, President
P.O. Box 146, Owings, MD 20736

www.usasurvival.org   443-964-8208

America's Survival, Inc.

America's Survival, Inc. (ASI) is a public policy organization with an established track record of fighting global Jihad, communism, and the United Nations. ASI President Cliff Kincaid, a former writer for Ronald Reagan's favorite newspaper, *Human Events,* is a journalist and media critic who first exposed Communist Party member Frank Marshall Davis as Barack Obama's mentor in February of 2008. He followed on May 22 of that year with a Washington, D.C. press conference which issued exclusive reports on Obama's communist connections in Hawaii and Chicago. In August of 2008, ASI released the 600-page FBI file on Davis. The *Washington Post* acknowledged that research from Cliff Kincaid and his associate, New Zealand blogger Trevor Loudon, "shaped the opinion of critics who believe Obama adopted radical, socialist ideologies" under the influence of Davis. Cliff's work has also appeared at Accuracy in Media, where he serves as Director of the AIM Center for Investigative Journalism.

ASI has an Internet-based Roku TV channel, produced in association with Jerry Kenney, which reaches people in 110 countries. Our YouTube channel has nearly 500 exclusive videos and one million views. We provide a free mobile device app for Android and iPhones to access our videos, news, and Facebook and Twitter feeds. ASI petition campaigns on national security issues reach over one million Americans a year.

Marxist Principles of Revolutionary Change

"In its rational form dialectics is a scandal and abomination to bourgeoisdom and its doctrinaire professors because it includes in its comprehension an affirmative recognition of the existing state of things, at the same time also the recognition of the negation of that state, of its inevitable breaking up; because it regards its inevitable breaking up; because it regards every historically developed social form as in fluid movement, and therefore takes into account its transient nature not less than its momentary existence; because it lets nothing impose upon it, and is in its essence critical and revolutionary."

- Karl Marx, *Capital,* Vol. 1, Moscow Foreign Language Publishing House, 1958, page 22.

"In October 1917 we parted with the old world, rejecting it once and for all. We are moving towards a new world, the world of Communism. We shall never turn off that road!"

- Mikhail Gorbachev, General Secretary of the Communist Party of the Soviet Union, "October and Perestroika: the Revolution Continues," November 2, 1987.

Table of Contents

Russia's Strategic Deception

This book reveals how Marxists think and act, and how to counteract them through a strategy called "dialectical reversal." It was used by President Ronald Reagan in his confrontation with the Soviet Union. We need to employ this strategy now to save our nation. International communism is not dead but more powerful and insidious than ever before. The term "political correctness" is sometimes used to describe the influence of cultural Marxism but the communist threat goes far beyond the manipulation of words, language, and values, and the exploitation of racial, ethnic, gender, or religious differences. It is international in scope and presents a direct military threat to the survival of the United States.

The common assumption is that communism is dead, and that President Obama is a traditional liberal, however misguided or incompetent. In fact, the evidence shows that President Obama has been a practicing Marxist since he was "schooled" in the ideology from the time he was a young man in Hawaii, under the mentorship of Communist Party operative Frank Marshall Davis, a suspected Soviet espionage agent. It's the ideology which has driven Obama during his two terms in office and now consumes Hillary Clinton and a significant portion of the Democratic Party.

The "Sword of Revolution," a term provided by the former intelligence agency official interviewed for this book, is the name for this superficially appealing ideology which purports to explain human history and offers "progress" through "struggle" to achieve "social justice." Lenin called dialectical materialism the "living soul" of Marxism, while Lin Biao, once heir apparent to Mao Zedong, called dialectics a "spiritual atom bomb," far superior to the real thing. It is the so-called "sharp weapon" of Marxism designed to usher in what the Marxists claim will be a heaven on earth but which actually figures to be a communist apocalypse on a global scale because of the nuclear threats posed by Russia, China, North Korea and Iran.

We are led to believe that Russia and China have abandoned communism, when the evidence assembled in this book proves otherwise. The former intelligence official we interviewed, who studied Marxist dialectics, has provided three essays on dialectical thinking that we have included near the end of this book. They are titled (1) Understanding Marxist Dialectics, (2) The Communist World Outlook, and (3) World Revolutionary Theory. His conclusion is that Russia and China are still communist and that world communism is still their goal.

What's more, both governments continue to support the communist North Korean regime, with its growing nuclear weapons program. "An estimated 3 million North Koreans have perished under North Korea's brutal dictatorial regime since the mid-1990s," notes the North Korea Freedom Coalition.[1] Chinese collaboration with North Korea even includes Chinese police who "hunt down and forcibly repatriate defectors to North Korea, where they face prison, torture, forced abortions and executions," notes a Washington Post review of several books on life in North Korea.[2] Former KGB officer Konstantin Preobrazhensky, a contributor to our book, *Back from the Dead: The Return of the Evil Empire,* says Russian President Vladimir Putin's relationship with the previous North Korean dictator, Kim Jong Il, was "held in strictest confidence, in order to keep Americans in the dark."[3]

Communist Cuba, given diplomatic recognition by the Obama Administration in a deal brokered by Pope Francis, is also implicated in support for the regime. A ship operated by a North Korean company was caught in 2013 carrying two Soviet fighter jets and weapons from Cuba to North Korea hidden under a cargo of sugar.

Russia has announced joint military exercises with North Korea, Cuba, Brazil and Vietnam.[4]

Globally, the Marxist view holds that the world moves through stages of development – slavery, feudalism, capitalism, socialism and communism. The role of the Marxists and the Communist Party is to accelerate this process of development, through class warfare and the exploitation of other differences, and to eliminate the "bourgeoisie" – the capitalist class – through any means necessary.

The Marxists see the U.S. as a society based on slavery which has since become the leading capitalist nation and must therefore be "transformed" into socialism on the road to communism.

The former intelligence official we interviewed for this book describes it this way:

> The game is a world "struggle" to determine which way of life is superior. It is principally developed by those supporting a political and economic philosophy demanding of them that they undertake a variety of methods and struggle to prove the supremacy of this ideology. In this game of world politics the rules have been drawn up by Marx, Engels, and Lenin, and further developed by the various "philosophers" of the Soviet Union, China, as well as the other socialist countries supporting the same worldview.

Our "way of life" is based on the principles set forth in the Declaration of Independence – the God-given rights to life, liberty, and the pursuit of happiness.

Marxists see a transition into world government on the way to world communism. That appears to be the current plan. The United Nations, established by a Soviet spy named Alger Hiss, who served as its first (acting) secretary-general, is an organization they are using to bring this about. It is no surprise that Obama has come to strongly rely on the United Nations in the Iran nuclear deal through secret side agreements with the organization's International Atomic Energy Administration (IAEA).

An examination of the endgame is contained in my books, *Global Bondage: The U.N. Plan to Rule the World* (1985) and *Global Taxes for World Government* (1987).[5] The Vatican's embrace of a "World Political Authority" and Pope Francis's endorsement of the global "climate change" agenda that is the subject of a United Nations conference in December makes a world government a real possibility for the first time in human history. The pope's acceptance of a "communist crucifix" from Marxist President Evo Morales of Bolivia starkly symbolizes the threat we face.

Vatican adviser Jeffrey Sachs, a proponent of abortion and other population control measures, has written in the Jesuit publication *America* that Pope Francis will directly challenge the "American idea" of God-given rights embodied in the Declaration of Independence. [6] This is what the Marxists are already doing with their dialectic of human "progress" that is based on materialism and atheism.

It is not clear if the pope is a dupe, an agent, or willing accomplice.

What we do know is that many have mistakenly assumed that the demise of the USSR meant the end of Soviet-style communism.

Soviet President Mikhail Gorbachev, in his 1987 book, *Perestroika*, explained what was coming to pass, if one understood dialectics. He wrote:

> The Leninist period is indeed very important. It is instructive in that it proved the strength of Marxist-Leninist dialectics, the conclusions of which are based on an analysis of the actual historical situation. The works of Lenin and his ideals of socialism remained for us an inexhaustible source of dialectical creative thought, theoretical wealth and political sagacity.

In other words, the intention was to restructure and reorganize within the communist system. Perestroika was the "negation of the negation" in dialectical terms.

Gorbachev cited two of the successful dialectical maneuvers of Lenin, The Brest-Litoysk Treaty with Germany in 1917, and the New Economic Policy of 1921. He said these decisions meant that Lenin was "guided by vital, not immediate, interests, the interests of the working class as a whole, of the Revolution and the future of socialism."

On the so-called "Sino-Soviet split," perhaps the most important dialectical maneuver in history, we consulted with the former intelligence official, who said:

The Sino-Soviet polemic which began in the early 1960's has had a profound effect on the foreign policies of non-communist countries since they have taken the appearance of great division between the two Communist giants, the USSR and the People's Republic of China, to be exactly what it appears to be and to conclude there are no unifying aspects between the two. What are the facts? Utilizing the communist world outlook the answer is that the relationships between the Soviets and the Chinese combine both factors of unity and division in a special way, a "dialectical way", and the appearance does not conform with the essence.

He goes on:

Can you imagine how the character of the Cold War could have changed had we understood dialectics and recognized they were simply using a method for which they had written the rules to deceive us while communicating with each other at the highest levels of the parties using dialectics? It was and is really an intellectual trick. I say this because it requires study to learn the method, and after that there is no trick.

Throughout the Cold War we were led by people who were Soviet experts and China experts, none of whom understood dialectics. They each dealt with their specialty as if there was no real interrelationship between the Soviet Union and China, and, to the extent they determined it did exist, their conclusion was that it was hostile. Moreover, in my conversation with people who were "experts" both in the CIA and State Department, they dismissed dialectics as philosophical thought with no practical value. Once that determination was made, there was then no need to study to confirm their position or reject it.

He then asks:

Can the apparent irreconcilable division perceived by Western analysts be the predominant feature of relations between the Chinese and the Soviets or can this very "division" be conducted, in a special way, a dialectical way, and, in fact, be used to promote unity between China and the Soviet Union thus strengthening the entire socialist camp?

That is, in fact, what has been happening in front of our eyes, as predicted by KGB defector Anatoliy Golitsyn, who said that the Sino-Soviet split was a charade to deceive the West. The former official told us:

Once they determined that our leaders and analysts would believe it [the Sino-Soviet "split"], the rest was easy – give the bourgeoisie what they expect to see – play up division in the communist world instead of unity. As a consequence, the communist world made huge gains during this period of the 'split.'

Despite the "collapse" of the USSR, Russia continues to serve as the base for world revolution.[7] President Vladimir Putin, a former colonel in the Soviet intelligence service, the KGB, created his own "United Russia" political party, but the Communist Party of Russia is still the second most powerful political party in the Russian Duma. In fact, Putin has praised Communist Party head Gennady Zyuganov as one of Russia's most influential politicians, and presented him with an early Soviet edition of the Communist Manifesto as a birthday gift. As the former intelligence official tells us, Putin and Zyuganov are both playing their respective and complementary roles, while leading some in the West to believe that Russia has abandoned its Soviet past.

As noted in Bill Gertz's book, *The China Threat*, Henry Kissinger "played the key role" in the talks that led President Nixon in 1972 to establish informal ties with China, and which ultimately led to formal diplomatic relations in 1979. Kissinger insisted that China had abandoned communism, and was no longer a threat. This was a major miscalculation based on willful ignorance of the Marxist-Leninist dialectic. Notra Trulock, the former Energy Department intelligence chief who blew the whistle on Chinese espionage in the U.S. nuclear weapons laboratories, subsequently wrote a book, *Code Name Kindred Spirit: Inside the Chinese Nuclear Scandal,* quoting Paul Redmond, former head of counterintelligence at the CIA, as saying that "millions of Americans" could someday die as a result of the Chinese communist theft of our nuclear secrets. Today, according to China policy expert Richard Fisher, China seeks military advantage over the U.S. through cyber espionage and hacking and a military buildup. [8]

In fact, as we discuss at length in this book, the Sino-Soviet "split" did not signify the worsening of political and ideological relations between these two major powers. Rather, it was an argument or "polemic" over the best road to take to world communism. China and Russia have taken different paths. The Sino-Soviet plan to dominate the world remains on track and the alliance between China and Russia has emerged openly on a global basis. The new book, *Russia-China Axis: The New Cold War and America's Crisis of Leadership,* by Douglas E. Schoen and Melik Kaylan, examines recent developments.

Communism is also very much alive in the United States. The late Larry Grathwohl, an FBI informant in the Weather Underground, disclosed that Bill Ayers and Bernardine Dohrn and their criminal gang had plans to eliminate as many as 25 million Americans if they came to power through "armed struggle" and terrorism. They later became college professors and political backers of Barack Obama.

There are literally dozens of Marxist and communist groups working in minority communities, on college campuses, and in society at large. They include:

- Democratic Socialists of America (which backed Obama's political career)
- Communist Party USA
- The Revolutionary Communist Party
- The League of Revolutionaries for a New America
- Socialist Workers Party
- Party for Socialism and Liberation
- Party of Communists, USA
- Labor United in Class Struggle
- U.S. Friends of the Soviet People
- Workers World Party

Some of the most important of these are the Communist Party USA, the Workers World Party (WWP) and the Party for Socialism and Liberation. They collaborate with the Russian, Chinese, North Korean, Cuban, and Iranian governments. In fact, the WWP was investigated by the House Internal Security Committee for its support of the North Korean regime and Arab terrorist groups. But the House Committee was disbanded by liberals in Congress. The WWP organized a 2014 Washington, D.C. pro-Castro event under the watchful eyes of José Ramón Cabañas, Chief of the Cuban Interests Section (and now the Embassy of Cuba). WWP operative Sara Flounders was a speaker at the 2014 "Rhodes Forum," which is sponsored by Vladimir Putin's close associate and former KGB official Vladimir

Yakunin. It is also known as the "World Public Forum Dialogue of Civilizations."

During the Vietnam War, official Congressional investigations discovered several of these Marxist groups, including the Communist Party USA, had involvement at a high-level in demonstrations against U.S. support for keeping South Vietnam free of communism.

Historically, these groups have concentrated on the "rights" of workers, considered to be the main group "oppressed" by the capitalists. In his final report for America's Survival, Inc., the late anti-communist researcher Herbert Romerstein noted that "Trade unions have always been the target of the communists. The plan was to capture the Trade Unions and use them to achieve communist goals." A pamphlet written by Lenin in 1920 entitled *"Left" Communism An Infantile Disorder* outlined the strategy and was published in every language and then distributed in June 1921 at the Third World Congress of the Communist International.

However, Robert Chandler, the late author of *Shadow World*, published in 2008, notes that we are today witnessing a new form of Marxism, based on the belief that "the problem with Karl Marx was that he was not Marxist enough."

He noted that Marx focused on workers when there were many others who could be considered "exploited" by the capitalist system. Added to the "workers" list from the twentieth century usage was a wide range of allegedly exploited individuals, including women, homosexuals, minorities, indigenous persons (Indians), immigrants, disabled persons, and animals.

The cause of "gay rights" was literally made up in America by a member of the Communist Party, Harry Hay. Recognized by homosexuals as the father of the modern gay rights movement, Hay was schooled in Marxism and Leninism and in fact taught these subjects as classes in Hollywood. [9] The endorsement of the "right" of homosexual marriage by the U.S. Supreme Court was a major victory for the Marxist movement in America. For example, the Party for Socialism and Liberation called it a "major legal victory" that promotes "the broader movement for LGBTQ liberation." LGBTQ means lesbian, gay, bisexual, transgender and "questioning" or "queer."

When agitation and political action don't work, violence, terrorism and mass murder can be justified as part of what the Marxists call the "struggle." Marxist National Lawyers Guild attorney Lynne Stewart, who was prosecuted and sentenced to 10 years in prison for violating the law against supporting terrorism, talked about the "diversity" of the various "liberation" movements, including the Puerto Rican Independence movement, the Black Liberation movement, the Native American struggle, the anti-Imperialist movement, and Earth and Animal Liberation movements.

The cause of "saving the Earth" has become one of the most popular Marxist causes these days since it is a vehicle for dismantling the capitalist system that is supposedly producing "global warming" or "climate change." It justifies the redistribution of wealth internationally, a longtime communist goal, in ways that appeal to liberals and those in favor of "social justice." In this campaign, Pope Francis has joined the bandwagon with an encyclical, *Laudato Si,* described by Catholic attorney Elizabeth Yore as "a Trojan Horse ready to attack and dismantle capitalism and replace it with one world order socialism." [10]

"After communism 'died,' environmentalism became the new communism," notes Catholic author Cornelia Ferreira during an appearance on America's Survival TV. Upon arriving at the Presidio in San Francisco to set up his Gorbachev Foundation, Mikhail Gorbachev also created the group known as Green Cross International to "ensure a sustainable and secure future." [11] That's Marxist jargon to justify a world government.

The "way in which they [the Communists] develop the struggle, internationally" can change because the "conditions" in the world change, the former intelligence official told us. Hence, new victims and "rights" can emerge at any time. Globally, the "conditions" also help explain China going through a capitalist stage and Russia officially dropping the Soviet label. But the idea that the communists have given up Marxism-Leninism is "erroneous," this former official contends. The goal is still world communism. Global environmentalism is merely the latest phase in this historical process, designed to confuse people about the ultimate goal.

Even while promoting the policy of "perestroika," or the restructuring of the Soviet state, Mikhail Gorbachev had declared, "We are moving towards a new world order, the world of communism. We shall never turn off that road." It's important to understand what really happened here. As I note in *Global Bondage*, John Lenczowski, former director of European and Soviet Affairs at the National Security Council, and Dr. J. Michael Waller, author of *Secret Empire*, contend that some of Gorbachev's reforms were authentic but that they went out of control, leading to the unintended disintegration of the Communist Party and the Soviet Union. Waller agrees, though, that Gorbachev never intended to weaken the KGB.

The former intelligence official told us that "perestroika" was "designed to accomplish a reorganization within the Soviet Union, in order to strengthen the position of the party and position within the World Communist Movement."

The problem for the Soviets, he says, was that Gorbachev "chose political organization over economic reorganization," and certain changes did not go as planned. As a result, the Soviet Union as an entity did go out of business and had to be reconstituted. What's important is that Russia and China have created new organizations, such as the

Shanghai Cooperation Organization (SCO), a group founded by Russia, China, Kyrgyzstan, Tajikistan and Uzbekistan. Another such international organization is the BRICS alliance of nations, incorporating Brazil, Russia, India, China, and South Africa. Brazil is a Marxist-run country in Latin America, where the advances of international communism have been striking.

Russian leader Vladimir Putin does not use the term "world communism" these days but there can be no doubt that Putin, trained in Marxism-Leninism by the KGB, the Soviet intelligence service, understands where the world is heading and what he is doing. Our book, *Back from the Dead: The Return of the Evil Empire,* examines how the remnants of Soviet communism are being preserved, even celebrated, in modern-day Russia.

U.S. political leaders don't even want to face up to the fact that the Marxists have already carried out political assassinations on American soil. Indeed, the assassinations of President John F. Kennedy and his brother, Robert F. Kennedy, are worth examining in some detail in terms of the communist threat and our inability to understand and cope with it. Both Kennedys were anti-communist liberals.

JFK assassin Lee Harvey Oswald was a communist member of the pro-Castro Fair Play for Cuba Committee and, after his arrest, tried to reach Communist Party USA attorney John Abt to act as his counsel. Oswald had traveled to the Soviet Union and had gone to the Cuban consulate in Mexico City on three occasions between September 27 and October 2, 1963, seeking a visa to travel to Cuba. During one of these visits, he proclaimed, "I'm going to kill Kennedy."

Nevertheless, the U.S. media have been flooded with claims about the CIA, right-wingers, or some other American group being behind the assassination. Ion Mihai Pacepa, the highest ranking intelligence official ever to defect from the Soviet bloc, says that, "For 15 years of my life at the top of the Soviet bloc intelligence community, I was involved in a world-wide disinformation effort aimed at diverting attention away from the KGB's involvement with Lee Harvey Oswald. The Kennedy assassination conspiracy was born—and it never died." Pacepa wrote the book, *Programmed to Kill: Lee Harvey Oswald, the Soviet KGB, and the Kennedy Assassination.*

Fidel Castro hated JFK for authorizing an invasion of Cuba and the overthrow of the Castro regime. Former CIA officer Brian Latell's book, *Castro's Secrets*, includes the revelation that Fidel Castro knew that Lee Harvey Oswald was going to kill President Kennedy.

During the "Cold War," Cuba hosted Soviet nuclear missiles targeting the U.S., and the Castro regime sponsored terrorism on American soil carried out by such groups as the Weather Underground and the Puerto Rican FALN. Cuba continues to protect anti-

American terrorists on the island such as Joanne Chesimard, a cop-killer who fled the U.S. with the help of the Weather Underground.

Sirhan Sirhan was a fanatical Palestinian Marxist who killed Robert F. Kennedy because Kennedy was a supporter of Israel. The assassination occurred on the first anniversary of the Six Day War in which Israel defeated the armies of its Arab neighbors. What's more, Sirhan's diaries include the repeated phrases, "RFK must die," and "long live communism."

Sirhan reportedly attended meetings of the Communist Party's W.E.B. Dubois Clubs and one of his closest friends was Walter Crowe, a communist who told investigators after the assassination that he feared that he may have influenced Sirhan to kill Kennedy.

The United States has always been the "main enemy" of the world communist movement and remains so today.

Internationally, with the Iran nuclear deal, brokered through the United Nations with the cooperation of Russia and China, it has become clear to many pro-Israel advocates that Barack Obama is operating as a conscious agent of anti-American forces.

The government of Israeli Prime Minister Netanyahu has been warning about Iran, a client state of Russia, while simultaneously conducting cordial relations with Russia and refusing to condemn Putin for

24

invading Ukraine. Israel and its defenders have to come to grips with the fact that Iran is a threat to the Jewish state, the region, and the world because of its Russian sponsorship.

The Iranian Ayatollah, Ali Khamenei, is KGB-trained, having been "educated" at the KGB's Patrice Lumumba University in Moscow. This means he is under Russian influence, if not an agent.

The Marxist view, as explained by the Party for Socialism and Liberation, is that the Obama deal is "an historic achievement for Iran," noting that it means that "regime-change has failed" and that Obama has guaranteed that the Iranian regime remains in place. According to the Marxist dialectic, this is "progress." It is on the same level as the Obama/Pope deal to recognize the communist regime in Cuba.

It is in the same context that we have to understand the significance of Obama's meeting with Nguyen Phu Trong, the head of Vietnam's Communist Party. Vietnam is one of the beneficiaries of Obama's proposed Trans-Pacific Partnership (TPP), a trade deal. If passed, it would benefit Vietnam's communist rulers.

Interestingly, Obama is trying to sell the agreement as a counter to China's influence throughout the world. He wants us to believe that China and Vietnam somehow differ on their common objective of achieving world communism at the expense of

America's standing as the leader of what used to be the Free World. However, the disagreements between China and Vietnam are of the "dialectical" variety and do not impinge on their common goal of world revolution and world communism. We have to keep in mind that both countries would gladly welcome the U.S. to help pay to accelerate the growth of their socialist economies and expand their markets. Russia used that strategy effectively after the "collapse" of the Soviet Union.

In addition to serving the interests of our enemies and adversaries, Marx said that global free trade would "create the impoverishment and class struggle necessary for economic chaos," notes analyst Nevin Gussack.[12] He explains that Marx saw that free trade "could serve as a revolutionary force that would break down the nation-state and due to competition from low wage labor, exacerbate the class differences between the bourgeoisie and proletariat." Marx famously noted in 1848 that, "...the protective system of our day is conservative, while the free trade system is destructive. It breaks up old nationalities and pushes the antagonism of the proletariat and the bourgeoisie to the extreme point. In a word, the free trade system hastens the social revolution. It is in this revolutionary sense alone, gentlemen, that I vote in favor of free trade."[13]

Global "free trade" agreements and international agencies which manage them have become essential parts of the "globalization" process to deindustrialize the United States, build up the economic and military capabilities of our enemies, and make a world government possible.

Mark Musser, a missionary in the former Soviet Union and expert on totalitarian movements, notes that Marx's conception of history was shaped by Georg Wilhelm Friedrich Hegel's (1770-1831) dialectical methodology.

Musser notes:

> In order to change the world, one must understand the laws of change. Marx was convinced that Hegel's dialectical methodology was the "logic of movement, of evolution, of change." Hegel declared that the root of all movement and change is contradiction. Contradictory movements within history clash with each other. The fallout of the collision produces a new higher synthesis which Hegel called the dialectic…Through the synthesis of antithetical contradictions, history not only develops, but it also progresses. History becomes a struggle, and it is through this struggle that improvement is made.

Musser notes that, "The communistic/socialistic cure has very often been worse than the capitalistic disease they are purportedly trying to ameliorate."

He is referring, of course, to the death toll of communism. *The Black Book of Communism* says

27

communism has already claimed 100 million lives. Going further, Professor Paul Kengor notes, "The latest research, for instance, claims that Mao Zedong alone was responsible for the deaths of at least 60-70 million in China, and ~~Joseph Stalin alone may well have killed 60 million in the USSR~~-those are just two communist countries that managed to far surpass the entire combined death toll of World War I and II, the two worst wars in the history of humanity."

In Russia and China, we saw how the Marxist dialectic leads to and justifies mass murder. In Cambodia, after Vietnam fell to the Communists, the Pol Pot regime killed about two million Cambodians, in what became known as the "killing fields."

As Vincent Cook argued in his article, "Pol Pot and the Marxist Ideal." the outcome was Marxism in action and represented "precisely what Marx predicted would be the ultimate culmination of all human history…" He explained, "Pol Pot has earned a special place in the history of Marxian Communism as his Khmer Rouge earned the special distinction of being the one Communist movement in history to actually attempt the full and consistent implementation of the ideals of Karl Marx."

The communist Revolutionary Armed Forces of Colombia (FARC) have been waging war against the government of Colombia for 50 years. More than 200,000 people have died. Now conducting "peace talks" with the government, the FARC has an office in Havana, Cuba, and has published a comic book for kids which hails its "great ideological leaders," including Lenin and Marx, and asks, "Who said communism died?" It pictures Uncle Sam being gored by a worker thrusting a hammer and sickle at him. "This is the right moment," the attacker proclaims.[14]

What the Marxists call "world communism" is actually an apocalypse that destroys the Western world, led by the United States, through a nuclear war if necessary.

In one of the essays in this book, the former intelligence agency official who studied Marxist dialectics says that "given the opportunities for serious error to arise through Western ignorance of communist methodology, and the tragic consequences which might ensue, a nuclear war, for example, it is indeed vital to Western policy makers that they understand Marxist-Leninist dialectics in order to insure that no cataclysmic event can take place which would have tragic consequences for all mankind."

Bucking the Obama Administration, top U.S. generals have recently and openly called Russia an "existential threat" to our survival as a nation.[15] A report from the National Institute for Public Policy says Russia has embarked on "a massive strategic modernization program to deploy new nuclear weapons and delivery systems." Not only that, but Russia has a ballistic missile defense to use against us.

Geopolitical analyst Jeff Nyquist, a contributor to our book, *Back from the Dead: The Return of the Evil Empire,* says the problem is not only the modernization of Russian offensive nuclear weapons but their development of defensive systems. "The Russians became angry and threatening when NATO tried to build a very modest missile defense system to stop an Iranian missile. Yet Russia has over 10,000 dual purpose surface-to-air/anti-ballistic missile SAM/ABMs for defense against our missiles and will be deploying a new ABM prototype next year," he says.

He adds, "Russia has potential war winning advantages over the U.S. and NATO—not necessarily in the number of nuclear weapons but in the number of its ABM batteries, and the upgrading of these batteries with a new generation of interceptor rockets while the American side makes no effort in this direction. The U.S. ABMs in Alaska and California would be lucky to stop 12 Russian warheads."

During an appearance on America's Survival TV, Nyquist praised our top generals, including Marine Corps General Joseph Dunford, chairman of the Joint Chiefs of Staff, for publicly describing Russia as an "existential threat." These warnings go against the official position of the Obama Administration.

Admiral William Gortney, who leads U.S. Northern Command, or NORTHCOM, has warned that the Russians are in the process of deploying long-range cruise missiles that can threaten our early warning radars and our ABM defenses in Alaska and California. On July 4th, America's Independence Day, Russian nuclear-capable bombers came within 40 miles of Alaska and California.

At one time, the Roman Catholic Church was a major force against international communism. Pope Pius XII had issued the "Decree Against Communism," excommunicating all Catholics collaborating with Communist organizations. His predecessor, Pope Pius XI, issued an encyclical on atheistic communism and explained that:

> Insisting on the dialectical aspect of their materialism, the Communists claim that the conflict which carries the world towards its final synthesis can be accelerated by man. Hence they endeavor to sharpen the antagonisms which arise between the various classes of society. Thus the class struggle with its consequent violent hate and destruction takes on the aspects of a crusade for the progress of humanity. On the other hand, all other forces whatever, as long as they resist such systematic violence, must be annihilated as hostile to the human race.[16]

Pope Pius XI was identifying the correlation of forces that are assembling right now to dominate the world and even destroy the United States and its allies in the process.

Obama's Role in World Revolution

Obama is a Marxist who sees his role in U.S. and world history as a major figure in the Marxist dialectic, bringing America from capitalism into socialism. It is also his mission to reduce our military capabilities while giving recognition and support to enemy regimes, such as Iran and Cuba, and preventing U.S. allies such as Ukraine from obtaining the weapons necessary to defend themselves against Russian aggression.

On May 22, 2008, working with the late Herbert Romerstein, the renowned communism expert, ASI held a Washington, D.C. news conference on "The Stealth Candidate," Barack Obama, and issued exclusive reports on his communist connections in Hawaii and Chicago. Later that year, in August, ASI released the 600-page FBI file on Obama's Communist Party mentor, Frank Marshall Davis, a suspected Soviet espionage agent. Subsequent revelations demonstrated that Davis was a pornographer and a pedophile.

Republican strategist Karl Rove, a paid Fox News contributor, had advised Republicans in 2008 and 2012 not to refer to Obama as a socialist. Yet, grassroots conservatives increasingly understand the dangers we face. We educate them through our international alternative news and information television channel, available on Roku and YouTube, called America's Survival TV. It is a real alternative to the increasingly politically-correct Fox News Channel.

In his 1995 book, *Dreams from My Father,* Barack Obama never discussed the identity of the mysterious "Frank" who had given him important advice on growing up black in what was described as a white racist world. We learned in 2008 that "Frank" was Frank Marshall Davis, a member of the Communist Party who was the subject of a 600-page FBI file. Still, the major media never asked Obama about this important relationship during his growing up years in Hawaii. The Drudge Report, a major source of information for conservatives, refused to run our advertising on the Obama-Davis link during the 2008 presidential campaign. Fox News ignored our revelations as well.

It was Gerald Horne, the John J. and Rebecca Moores Chair of History and African American Studies at the University of Houston, who first publicly revealed the Obama-Davis link. He spoke at a March 23, 2007, event at New York University's Tamiment Library to celebrate the donation of Communist Party materials to the library. A contributor to Communist Party USA publications such as *Political Affairs* magazine, Horne, speaking before an audience that included Communist Party leaders, discussed then-Senator Barack Obama's relationship with Davis, who died in 1987.

In that 2007 speech at Tamiment Library, entitled, "Rethinking the History and Future of the Communist

Party," Horne had referred to Davis as "an African-American poet and journalist" who was "certainly in the orbit of the CP—if not a member …" and had become a friend to Barack Obama and his family in Hawaii. Horne also noted that Obama, in his memoir, spoke "warmly of an older black poet, he identifies simply as 'Frank' as being a decisive influence in helping him to find his present identity as an African-American…"

The Horne speech was subsequently published in the Communist Party (CPUSA) newspaper *People's World.*

In a June 2015 interview over America's Survival TV on Roku and YouTube, Horne said he came across the activities of Davis while researching his book on labor unions in Hawaii, *Fighting in Paradise: Labor Unions, Racism and Communists in the Making of Modern Hawaii.* "So as I was reading about Frank Marshall Davis there was the simultaneous ascension to influence of then-Senator Barack Obama and I read his memoir [Dreams from My Father], where he talks about a character by the name of Frank and I just put two and two together," Horne told me. "I don't think it took a great logical leap." He added, "The press should have uncovered this, not some obscure professor in Houston."

In an extraordinary development, video of Obama explicitly and openly identifying "Frank" as Frank Marshall Davis suddenly surfaced on the Internet in March of 2015. The footage was said to have been recorded on September 20, 1995, with the program originally airing on Channel 37 Cambridge Municipal Television as an episode of the show, "The Author Series." It's not clear how many saw this program when it aired. In the video, Obama is introduced as a Harvard Law School student and President of the Harvard Law Review.

By August of 2015, our own America's Survival TV video on this development, titled, "Obama Admits Communist 'Schooled' him on White Racism," had been seen over 359,000 times. It demonstrates a hunger for understanding the significance of the Obama presidency and the true nature of the Marxist movement of which he is a part.

Racism was the hook that got Obama into the Marxist movement. Like Davis, it looks like Obama does see Marxism as the answer to white racism. And that helps explain why the true identity of "Frank" was concealed during Obama's run for the presidency.

Alan Keyes, a black conservative who ran against Barack Obama for the Senate in 2004, had exposed Obama as a Marxist back then. At an America's Survival, Inc. conference on cultural Marxism in April of 2015, he explained the importance of the God-given rights set forth in the Declaration of Independence – life, liberty, and the pursuit of happiness. This is not only our defense against Marxism but a form of "dialectical reversal" to use against our enemies for psychological and political reasons.

Obama showed his true self while campaigning in 2008 when he told a well-heeled gathering of liberals that he was having trouble winning over white working-class voters in Pennsylvania and the Midwest. He said "it's not surprising…that they get bitter, they cling to guns or religion or antipathy to people who aren't like them or anti-immigrant sentiment or anti-trade sentiment as a way to explain their frustrations."

Whites have always been a special target for Obama since they are associated with colonialism, capitalism and the oppression of minority groups. His associates, communists Bill Ayers and Bernardine Dohrn, had explicitly named whites as the target in their book, *Race Course Against White Supremacy.*

Professor Paul Kengor wrote a book about Obama's deep relationship with Davis, [17] but said that it is a "riddle" as to "how much of the Davis worldview—about the world, its events, and the dialectic of history—was passed on to Obama."

It is a riddle in the sense that Obama doesn't admit or talk about his Marxist outlook. But the Marxists count Obama as one of their own. Frank Chapman, a CPUSA supporter, had written a letter to the party newspaper hailing the Illinois senator's victory in the Iowa caucuses during the 2008 presidential campaign. "Obama's victory was more than a progressive move; it was a dialectical leap ushering in a qualitatively new era of struggle," Chapman wrote. "Marx once compared revolutionary struggle with the work of the mole, who sometimes burrows so far beneath the ground that he leaves no trace of his movement on the surface. This is the old revolutionary 'mole,' not only showing his traces on the surface but also breaking through."

An authority on Marxism and the dialectical view of history, Horne had said in that speech at Tamiment Library, "At some point in the future, a teacher will add to her syllabus Barack's memoir and instruct her students to read it alongside Frank Marshall Davis' equally affecting memoir, 'Living the Blues' and when that day comes, I'm sure a future student will not only examine critically the Frankenstein monsters that U.S. imperialism created in order to subdue Communist parties but will also be moved to come to this historic and wonderful archive in order to gain insight on what has befallen this complex and intriguing planet on which we reside."

A big part of this approach is the exploitation of racial differences.

Although Obama is black, most of the communist groups active in American society are led by whites. The late Larry Grathwohl, former FBI informant in the Weather Underground, understood from personal experience how white communists exploited blacks and other minority groups. Discussing the significance of that 2009 book by Bill Ayers and Bernardine Dohrn entitled, *Race Course Against White Supremacy,* Grathwohl said Ayers and Dohrn, who are white, always regarded Barack Obama, whose political career they sponsored, as a tool—a puppet—to use against white America.

Grathwohl understood the role that blacks were to play in the revolution when he was assigned to Detroit, Michigan, in order to bomb a police station. Shortly after his arrival there in late January of 1970, he was assigned to a cell with four other people, and during a meeting with Bill Ayers they were told "that our objective would be to place bombs at the Detroit Police Officers Association (DPOA Building) and at the 13th precinct."

The DPOA building, Grathwohl discovered, was a converted single-family brownstone that had been built prior to World War II. Next to the DPOA building was a Red Barn restaurant, located in a predominantly black neighborhood, meaning that most of the customers were black.

"After a week of information gathering we had another meeting with Bill Ayers and at this time I suggested to Bill that if we placed the bomb in the walkway between these two buildings, the DPOA building would suffer little if any damage while the Red Barn restaurant would most likely be destroyed. I also concluded that customers in that restaurant would die."

He said Ayers told him, "Sometimes innocent people have to die in a revolution." Grathwohl said, "I was shocked. I couldn't believe that a person who had so eloquently spoken of the black liberation movement could be so callous when it was obvious that the resulting explosion would kill many of the people he claimed to be so concerned about."

The former official we interviewed about the subject of dialectics says that Obama speaks in dialectical terms such as when he talks about "the people." He explained:

> He has two meanings. One is the general expression he uses and which he lets the masses assume means virtually all Americans. The other side of the same expression is when a revolutionary talks of "the people" he really is using Lenin and Mao's definition. "The people" are those who support the revolution or, in this case, Obama's positions, and everyone else is the enemy of the revolution and must eventually be eliminated or the revolution can't succeed. So, when Obama, or any other competent revolutionary speaks to "the people" the general population likely will interpret it one way while revolutionary elements will take it in its dual meaning--one meaning for the general population and what it means in the revolutionary sense.

This former official explained Obama's "transformation" of the U.S. domestically:

> Obama wants to transform the system. Initially he has three obstacles to overcome

(assuming he doesn't want a violent or revolutionary transformation). He has to dominate the executive branch. One can see from his appointment of czars, some of whom are admitted Marxists, others with strong socialist tendencies compatible with the Marxists, so he is essentially in control here. Then he has to transform the judiciary and the legislative branches. He has already made an impact in the judiciary by appointing some judges with very liberal social views--or more. He now has two appointees on the Supreme Court. So, in the judiciary he is developing a cadre that is likely to find in his favor in cases that interest him. The last one is the legislative. This is the toughest nut for him to crack and is the one which stands in his way for a complete transformation.

"As the leader of the nation," comments Alexander Markovsky, a Russian émigré who studied Marxism-Leninism in the former Soviet Union, "the president is expected to govern by constitutional principles and political consensus. Obama, however, unable and unwilling to secure hegemony through consent, has been acting as a Marxist guerrilla leader who hates political opponents and seeks imposition of his agenda by a combination of force, coercion, and emotional mass appeal. As a consequence, instead of being a symbol of national unity, he has fostered a condition of civil war." [18]

Markovsky further comments, "In the world of Marxist dialectical materialism, change is the product of a constant conflict between opposites, arising from the internal contradictions inherent in all events, ideas, and movements. Therefore, any significant change in a society, according to Marxism, must be accompanied by a period of upheaval."

Lenin had said, "Our task is to utilize every manifestation of discontent, and to collect and utilize every grain of rudimentary protest."

Markovsky comments, "Indeed, if you want to change a society, here is Lenin's script: cause the problem. Spread the misery. Send a cadre of professional community organizers to unite all of the angry and disinherited spirits to fuel an organized revolt. Entice chaos and violence. Exploit chaos for larger political objectives. Blame your political opponents, demonize and criminalize them."

Debra Rae, a Christian author and radio talk show host, has studied how dialectical theory has undermined the notion of fixed rights and wrongs, resulting in a paradigm shift that has "arguably shattered the essential foundation of Western culture." [19] The shift is from absolute truth to relative truth, from knowledge-based decisions and conscience to "consensus." This has occurred in such areas as the nature of the family and national sovereignty giving way to globalism. "Total transformation of society and total transformation of the world is what they're looking for," she says.

Edward Hunter, a foreign correspondent and specialist in propaganda warfare, testified before the House Committee on Un-American Activities, "We now confuse moral standards with the sophistication of dialectical materialism, with a Communist crackpot theology which teaches that everything changes, and that what is right or wrong, good or bad, changes as well. So nothing they say is really good or bad. There is no such thing as truth or a lie; and any belief we actually held was simply our being unsophisticated. They don't say this in so many words, except to those who are already indoctrinated in communism. What they do say to the rest of us is to be objective; and then they twist that word 'objective' into meaning what they mean by dialectical materialism."

But rather than being a "crackpot theory," as he called it in his testimony in 1958, Marxist dialectics has been accepted by many under the banner of "political correctness," a form of special deference to "victim" groups, and the blind acceptance of radical social change as somehow the wave of the future. The Marxists were more successful than Hunter ever imagined. Even Fox News has been criticized for its politically correct approach.[20]

Former Florida Governor Jeb Bush's speech that launched his presidential campaign noted that Hillary Clinton's "progressive agenda" includes the admonition that traditional religious beliefs "have to be changed." Mrs. Clinton's entire quote, in talking about opposition to her version of feminism and demands for abortion, was that "…deep-seated cultural codes, religious beliefs and structural biases have to be changed." Bush said of the Democrats, "They have offered a progressive agenda that includes everything but progress."

But the Marxist notion of dialectical "progress" is not real progress, as ordinary people understand the term. It includes the planned disintegration of the traditional family structure that has been the basis of Western civilization. Kengor, author of the book, *Takedown: From Communists to Progressives, How the Left Has Sabotaged Family and Marriage*, told me in an interview that the progressives are guided by the belief that "new rights are coming all the time and that everything is in a state of evolution." He added, "There are no absolutes for them." Hence, the gay rights movement has now morphed into rights for so-called transgenders, as we see in the relentless media propaganda that is designed to convince the public that men can, and perhaps should, become women. Kengor says the next step is for "progress" or "evolution" to a new level that includes such concepts and arrangements as multiple wives, group marriages, sibling marriages, fathers and stepfathers marrying daughters and stepdaughters, and uncles marrying nieces.

Under the approach of the Marxist dialectic, the Supreme Court's legalization of abortion in 1973 justified the destruction of the rights of the unborn in the name of the "women's rights" conferred on what

Marxists consider an oppressed group. The Marxists have not only celebrated the feminist "right" to abortion but in China have required that women have abortions, for the sake of the one-child policy mandated by the Communist government.

Cornelia Ferreira says the feminist movement removed women from the family and their traditional roles as wife and mother in the name of their "emancipation," a deception which served communist purposes.[21] One of America's leading feminists, Bella Abzug, was a pro-Soviet member of several Communist Party fronts. Abzug regarded women as another "exploited" group to be used to further the Marxist agenda. [22]

Decades before the legalization of abortion in the U.S., ex-Communist Whittaker Chambers would explain how the abortion mentality was the communist mentality. Chambers, who had exposed top State Department official and United Nations founder Alger Hiss as a Communist agent, said, "Abortion was a commonplace of party life. There were Communist doctors who rendered that service for a small fee...Abortion, which now fills me with physical horror, I then regarded, like all Communists, as a mere physical manipulation."

In the politically correct or Marxist atmosphere, however, the destruction of innocent unborn lives has been replaced by a fictitious "war on women" label that is pinned on pro-life conservatives who promote motherhood.

Reagan's "Dialectical Reversal" Strategy

President Ronald Reagan understood Marxism because he had fought the Communists in Hollywood. He fought them on the global level as well. In his Westminster Speech to member of the British Parliament on June 8, 1982, he challenged the Marxist philosophy, as represented by the Soviet Union, with a direct attack. He said:

> In an ironic sense Karl Marx was right. We are witnessing today a great revolutionary crisis, a crisis where the demands of the economic order are conflicting directly with those of the political order. But the crisis is happening not in the free, non-Marxist West, but in the home of Marxist-Leninism, the Soviet Union. It is the Soviet Union that runs against the tide of history by denying human freedom and human dignity to its citizens.

The system which guarantees human freedom and dignity to its citizens is based on the U.S. Declaration of Independence and the God-given rights to life, liberty, and the pursuit of happiness.

In their book on the Reagan speech at Westminster, Robert C. Rowland and John M. Jones commented:

> Reagan's address at Westminster is best understood as a thoroughgoing subversion of the rationale for communism and a defense of liberal democracy organized around three

levels of dialectical reversal: historical development, ideological engagement, and language systems. Since Marx, advocates of communism have argued that a world revolution resulting in the creation of a worker's paradise was inevitable on historical grounds. Proponents also argued for the superiority of communism as an ideological system in competition with liberal democracy and created a terminology based primarily in metaphor supporting the inevitability of their historical and. ideological victory. Reagan's address at Westminster was organized around dialectical reversal on all three grounds. Using this rhetorical tactic, Reagan built a strong case that communism was a bankrupt worldview and that the power of' the liberal democratic idea would ultimately triumph over communism. Given the 'dialectical character' of Marxist thought, Reagan's threefold subversion of it functioned to fundamentally negate the power of the ideology.[23]

Reagan was addressing the dialectical process, as carried out by the communists on a global basis. This notion of "dialectical reversal" is absolutely critical. One weapon he used against the Marxists was humor. A Ronald Reagan joke, reportedly told to Mikhail Gorbachev, was about two men walking down a street in Moscow, when one asks, "Is this pure communism? Have we passed through the stage of socialism and reached pure communism?" The other replies, "Hell, no. It's gonna get a lot worse."

Malachi Martin's book, *The Keys of This Blood,* examined this conflict on a global level. Martin wrote about how Pope John Paul II, the anti-communist pope, was resisting the Marxist surge and countered it with the "Culture of Life." Pope John Paul II had worked closely with the Reagan administration in opposition to communism and the global population control movement. He once complained that a U.N. conference on population issues was designed to "destroy the family" and was the "snare of the devil."

Tragically, Pope Francis has embraced the Marxist, secular and New Age movements that Pope John Paul II had opposed. Francis even had a warm meeting with Putin, who was a KGB colonel, despite the fact that the 1981 assassination attempt on Pope John Paul II was blamed on the KGB. [24]

Accuracy in Media founder Reed Irvine's longtime assistant, Bernard Yoh, was an anti-communist fighter and expert on psychological warfare. He wrote a powerful pamphlet, "A Handbook for Survival," arguing that one reason for the advance of communism was "cowardice on the part of the Free World." Ideologically, he said, the responsibility for saving the free world "rests squarely on the Christians."

That means, in the current context, pushing back against the Vatican alliance which has emerged not only with the United Nations but with Vladimir Putin's Russia and the Russian Orthodox Church, an institution long dominated by the Soviet and now Russian intelligence service. Michael Hichborn of the Lepanto Institute has done amazing work exposing links between the highest levels of the Roman Catholic Church and an international communist group known as the World Social Forum. He has also published a comparison of the U.N.'s Sustainable Development Goals (SDGs) and communist objectives. [25]

Despite major setbacks for the United States in foreign affairs under Obama, three countries – Colombia, Ukraine, and Egypt -- stand as success stories against the forces of international communism and Islamism. In Colombia, the population has backed the government in a war that defeated an armed Marxist revolution. In Ukraine, Lenin statues have been toppled across the country and the government is now trying to "de-communize" the society. Egypt has banned Al Jazeera and the Muslim Brotherhood, while Egypt's President Abdel Fattah el-Sisi delivered a dramatic speech urging Islamic leaders to reform the religion of Islam to eliminate terrorist elements.

Reagan conceived what became known as the "Reagan Doctrine" of supporting anti-communist freedom fighters in such places as Nicaragua. His policies resulted in the defeat of the Nicaraguan Sandinista communists, and the collapse of the communist terrorist movement in neighboring El

Salvador. But the communists never gave up. The pro-communist association called the São Paulo Forum was created in 1990, after the collapse of the Soviet Union led many to believe communism itself was on the wane. However, that was when Fidel Castro reached out to Luiz Inácio Lula de Silva of the Workers' Party of Brazil, who would later become President of Brazil. An event was hosted in São Paulo, Brazil, bringing together what came to be known as the São Paulo Forum. The international movement included many different leftist groups, such as the communist narco-terrorists known as the Revolutionary Armed Forces of Colombia (FARC), and communist and leftist parties in the region.

Although the communists made significant advances, they are today facing a backlash in many countries. In Brazil, President Dilma Rousseff is coming under tremendous pressure to resign her presidency. Millions have demanded the impeachment of Rousseff, a former Marxist terrorist, and the end of the rule of the Brazilian Workers' Party.

Brazilian philosopher Olavo de Carvalho, President of the Inter-American Institute for Philosophy, Government, and Social Thought, said about his country: "Never and nowhere has a government been so completely rejected by its own population. But it is more than that. It is not only the rejection of a government, or a President. It is the rejection of the whole system of power that has been created by the Workers' Party, which includes intellectuals and opinion-makers in the big media. People are no longer afraid of going against the Workers' Party. Brazilians realized that all the power that President Lula, President Rousseff, and their minions had was based on a bluff, and now they are calling it."

The protests in Brazil are giving hope to those who see an opportunity to defeat Marxism in the Western hemisphere.

The Bush administration ultimately failed in its effort to foment democracy in the Middle East, in part because Obama abandoned the effort in Iraq. However, the Bush Administration succeeded in helping the Colombian government of President Alvaro Uribe in its war with the Cuban-backed FARC. William Scoggins, counter-narcotics program manager at the U.S. military's Southern Command, called the NSA's help in locating and killing at least two dozen leaders of communist terrorist movements in Colombia a "game changer" that decimated the organization. But Uribe's successor, President Juan Manuel Santos, the former defense minister, suddenly opened up negotiations with the FARC in Havana. The Santos-led negotiations could enable the FARC to escape criminal charges and emerge in the political process in Colombia as a respectable opposition movement. It was a dialectical move on the part of the FARC that has Obama's approval.

A report had appeared on March 1, 2008, before U.S. presidential elections, indicating an Obama link to the FARC. Operation Phoenix had been launched by Colombian special security forces just inside the

Ecuadorian border. Raúl Reyes, second in command of the FARC, was killed. Documents found in Reyes' computer after his death disclosed that "gringos" representing Obama wanted to meet with the FARC and that they were opposed to U.S. military aid for the Colombian government. Obama had been publicly critical of the Colombia government's human rights record.

On March 21, 2015, ASI participated in the Washington Conclave for Democracy at the National Press Club in Washington, D.C. The main goal of the Conclave was to promote free and transparent elections in Latin America, where democratic institutions are weak, such as in Venezuela, Brazil, Ecuador, Bolivia, El Salvador and Nicaragua. It was also designed to expose fraud and deception in the electoral processes in countries such as Venezuela and Brazil.

Alejandro Peña Esclusa, a Venezuelan political figure, created UnoAmerica, an anti-communist alliance, to oppose efforts to spread Marxist revolution in Venezuela and throughout the region.[26]

We need first-rate intelligence agencies, including the CIA and the National Security Agency, to understand these developments, support freedom, and plan to undermine our enemies. As the former intelligence official told us, one key problem is the failure or unwillingness to understand Marxist dialectics:

...in my conversation with people who were "experts" both in the CIA and State Department, they dismissed dialectics as philosophical thought with no practical value. Once that determination was made, there was then no need to study to confirm their position or reject it.

Another part of this unfolding tragedy is how Edward Snowden, the former NSA and CIA contract employee still based in Moscow, is being hailed as a whistleblower in the United States by liberals and some conservatives. Ronald Reagan biographer Craig Shirley has even rallied to Snowden's defense. What Shirley and other Snowden supporters ignore is the fact that the NSA's surveillance activities rely mostly on a Ronald Reagan Executive Order (12333) and that funding and manpower for the NSA increased dramatically under Reagan.

In fact, President Reagan used the NSA to undermine America's enemies, especially the old USSR.

National security reporter Bill Gertz wrote in 2013 about how a former "top-secret" document, "United States Cryptologic History, Series VI, Vol. 5: American Cryptology During the Cold War, 1945-89," contained a section on how President Ronald Reagan realized the value of the NSA's unique electronic intelligence collection capabilities.

The history notes that "the best known exposure of SIGINT [signals intelligence] since the Pearl Harbor hearings of 1945 had actually come in 1983, when the Reagan administration played the intercepted cockpit conversations of the Soviet pilot as he shot down KAL-007. The SIGINT gave the administration a tremendous foreign policy coup."

On September 1, 1983, the Soviet Union shot down the civilian airliner KAL-007, killing 269 people.

In 1986, the document states, Reagan became the first American president to visit the NSA, as he gave the official dedication speech for the NSA's two new buildings. He wanted to loosen "the legal reins governing intelligence," the document says, giving rise to Reagan executive order 12333. It gave the NSA latitude in SIGINT collection that the agency had not had during the disastrous Carter years.

This executive order remains in effect. Not even Obama has tried to revoke it.

Based on this history, one would have to conclude that President Reagan would defend the NSA. The tragedy is that, with Obama in office rather than a conservative like Reagan, some conservatives decided to join the campaign to undermine the agency that Reagan considered absolutely essential to America's security and survival.

The revelations in the ASI book on Snowden, *Blood on His Hands: The True Story of Edward Snowden*, have been confirmed by the New York Times, which reported on July 20, 2015, that, "The Islamic State has also studied revelations from Edward J. Snowden, the former National Security Agency contractor, about how the United States gathers information on militants. A main result is that the group's top leaders now use couriers or encrypted channels that Western analysts cannot crack to communicate, intelligence and military officials said." The "Report of the Independent Surveillance Review" from the Royal United Services Institute for Defense and Security Studies in Britain cites a video released onto a jihadist platform which "outlined what they had learned from the Snowden disclosures, providing advice on how to avoid detection and listing software packages that protect against surveillance."

A new security-conscious president will need an NSA capable of gathering the intelligence information the nation needs to defend itself. Time is running out.

Marxists and New Agers in the Democratic Party

Barack Obama is only one of many Marxists on the scene today. Hillary Clinton is another. Plus, there are dozens operating within the Democratic Party, masquerading under the banner of the Congressional Progressive Caucus. My friend and associate, Trevor Loudon, has spent many years analyzing them. He wrote *The Enemies Within: Communists, Socialists and Progressives in the US Congress,* which is now being made into a major film.[27]

President Reagan complained about communist influence in Congress back in the 1980s. In 1987 Arnaud de Borchgrave asked President Reagan what can be done "when two dozen pro-Marxists with real political clout can, in our own Congress, influence great issues of defense, arms control and international policy?" Reagan agreed that this was, indeed, "a problem we have to face," and that the Soviets and their communist agents had tried to "make anti-communism unfashionable. And they have succeeded." He then made a reference to the days when Congress had a committee (the House Committee on Un-American Activities) that would investigate even its own members if communist involvement was suspected. We need such a committee today.

The Members of Congress for Peace through Law, a group which was instrumental in the betrayal of South Vietnam to Communism, eventually grew to become the Congressional Progressive Caucus, the largest group of congressional members within the Democratic Party. The only Senate member of the Congressional Progressive Caucus is Vermont's "independent" Senator Bernie Sanders, who votes with Senate Democrats.

Mrs. Clinton is coming across on the Democratic side looking like a moderate, by virtue of the fact that Sanders, an open socialist, is running "to her left" for the Democratic presidential nomination. The Clinton-Sanders show has all the earmarks of a carefully staged demonstration of the Marxist dialectic, an exercise designed to create the appearance of conflict in order to force even more radical change on the American people through Democratic Party rule. Only the Marxist insiders seem to understand what is happening.

Mrs. Clinton is a student of Saul Alinsky, the pro-Marxist organizer whose book, *Rules for Radicals*, was originally dedicated to Satan. Mrs. Clinton's thesis on Alinsky for Wellesley College was titled "There Is Only the Fight..." It is the Alinsky version of the Marxist dialectic. Of course, it was also adopted by Obama, who was trained by Alinsky disciples working with the Catholic Church in Chicago.

Barbara Olson had come to the conclusion while researching her book on Hillary, *Hell to Pay,* that "she has a political ideology that has its roots in Marxism."

The Sanders candidacy actually makes Hillary look like a moderate while she moves further to the left, a place she wants to be, in response to the left-wing Democratic base.

As for Sanders, if any member of Congress should be investigated and even under surveillance by the NSA, he is the one. During the 1980s he collaborated with Soviet and East German "peace committees" to stop President Reagan's deployment of nuclear missiles in Europe, in order to counter a massive Soviet strategic nuclear advantage. Sanders had openly joined the Soviets' "nuclear freeze" campaign to undercut Reagan's military build-up.

Bernie Sanders, then identified as former mayor of Burlington, Vermont, even showed up on a list of speakers at a 1989 U.S. Peace Council event to "end the Cold War" and "fund human needs." Other speakers at the U.S. Peace Council event included Rep. John Conyers, a Democrat from Michigan; Gunther Dreifahl of the East German "Peace Council;" Jesse Jackson aide Jack O'Dell; and Palestine Liberation Organization (PLO) official Zehdi Terzi.

Congressional hearings in 1982 demonstrated that the U.S. Peace Council was affiliated with the Soviet-controlled World Peace Council and run by the Communist Party USA. It was part of what the FBI called the Soviet "active measures" apparatus, designed to discredit the U.S. and support communist objectives.

As for Hillary, Barbara Olson reported in her book that Robert Borosage, who served as director of the Marxist Institute for Policy Studies (IPS), was "a colleague and close acquaintance" of Clinton. Olson wrote that Mrs. Clinton operated in the "reaches of the left including Robert Treuhaft and Jessica Mitford," who had been "committed Communists" and "Stalinists." Olson said that Hillary worked for Treuhaft and paved the way for Mitford to lobby then-Governor Bill Clinton on the death penalty issue.

Olson described Hillary as a "budding Leninist" who understood the Leninist concept of acquiring, accumulating and maintaining political power at any cost. She wrote that "Hillary has never repudiated her connection with the Communist movement in America or explained her relationship with two of its leading adherents." Olson, of course, was the lawyer and conservative commentator who was murdered by Islamic terrorists when the aircraft she was on, American Airlines Flight 77, was hijacked and flown into the Pentagon in the September 11, 2001, attacks. The crash killed 125 people on the ground and another 64 passengers and crew.

Researcher Carl Teichrib provided me with a photo of a Hillary meeting with Cora Weiss from the May 2000 edition of "Peace Matters," the newsletter of the Hague Appeal for Peace. Weiss, a major figure in the Institute for Policy Studies, gained notoriety for organizing anti-Vietnam War demonstrations and traveling to Hanoi to meet with communist leaders. In the photo, Hillary is shown fawning over a Hague Appeal for Peace gold logo pin that Weiss is wearing.

Teichrib, editor of *Forcing Change*, was an observer at the 1999 World Federalist Association (WFA) conference, held in association with the Hague Appeal for Peace. In the WFA booklet, "The Genius of Federation: Why World Federation is the Answer to Global Problems," the group described how a "world federation," a euphemism for world government, could be achieved by advancing "step by step toward global governance," mostly by enhancing the power and authority of U.N. agencies.

Clinton and Sanders are also staging a competition for votes from the so-called New Age Movement, a major and increasingly important constituency in the Democratic Party. Constance Cumbey notes, "There are three major aspects of the New Age Movement: a New World Order, a New World Religion, and a messianic figure to head both. Its toolbox is mysticism, in effect 'altered states of consciousness.' You may hear it described as 'meditation.'" She adds, "Socialism and New Age beliefs are almost inextricably linked."

When she was First Lady, Clinton held a "channeling" session or voodoo-like séance arranged by Jean Houston of the Foundation for Mind Research, in order to "communicate" with the spirit of Eleanor Roosevelt.

Sanders has his own New Age adviser by the name of Marianne Williamson, a "spiritual teacher" whose books have become best-sellers thanks to recommendations from Oprah Winfrey. Williamson, who unsuccessfully ran for the Democratic nomination for Congress in 2014 as a "progressive" advocate for abortion and homosexual rights, and socialized health care, writes on the Sanders for president website about the need for "revolutionary power."

Sanders spoke at one of her "Sister Giant" conferences, along with Thom Hartmann, the "progressive" radio and TV host who is featured on the Moscow-financed propaganda channel known as Russia Today or RT. [28] His RT show promoted Sanders and asked "Will Bernie Be the Beginning of a Revolution?"

Like Sanders, Williamson is considered by some to be pro-Israel. But in her book, *The Healing of America,* she discussed how Egypt's highest Muslim cleric had once approached her "to make sure you understand that Islam is a religion of peace." She didn't say whether the Muslim leader condemned and rejected the passages in the Koran that call for killing the "Infidels" who resist Islam. She also wrote, "The creative challenge of spiritual life is to know enough about God to be hopeful. From Jesus to Buddha to Moses to Mohammed, wayshowers have risen out of the timeline of history to draw maps and pave roads to a more perfect world." The comparison of Jesus, who led a perfect life and preached love, to the

Muslim Prophet Mohammad, is offensive on its face. Islam began in violence and Mohammad himself was a violent warrior, even a terrorist.

Williamson works closely with Rep. Keith Ellison, a "progressive" Muslim Democratic Congressman who wrote the foreword to a book entitled *Green Deen: What Islam Teaches about Protecting the Planet,* about a close relationship between Islam and modern environmentalism. Ellison is co-chair of the Congressional Progressive Caucus.

The "revolution" apparently includes occultists as well as Islamists. Williamson describes being part of an "interfaith ceremony at the United Nations chapel," which is actually a "Meditation Room" in the U.N. building where officials go to have mystical experiences. The place features a huge slab of black granite, a piece of "modern art" on the wall, and strange lights.

Williamson follows in the tradition of former Democratic Vice President Al Gore, who participated in the 1992 U.N.-sponsored Earth Summit and has written openly about the Earth having sacred qualities. He has praised primitive pagan religions and goddess worship. Those involved in what has been called the Cult of Gaia, named for an alleged Earth spirit, believe in a form of spiritual planetary consciousness. The U.N. Environmental Program once promoted the idea of an "Environmental Sabbath," encouraging children to hold hands around a tree and meditate.

Russia's Power Grab in Europe

The term "Red-Green" has been used by investigative journalist Jim Simpson to describe the invasion of the United States by legal and illegal immigrants from the Middle East and Latin America.[29] The term also describes the threat of Islamist terrorism secretly sponsored by Russia.

The seemingly esoteric subject matter of "Marxist dialectics" holds the key to analyzing not only a resurgent Russia and the Russia-China alliance, but Russian-supported Islamic terrorism. ASI held an entire conference on Russian support for Islamic terrorism, the proceedings of which are available at www.LeninandSharia.com

In his report for that conference, former KGB officer Konstantin Preobrazhensky noted:

> The communists have considered Islam their ally from the very beginning, because in the early 20th century, Islam was the religion of the "oppressed people." Support of Islam was considered a part of Russian-based anticolonialism. It is very significant that Vladimir Lenin in December 1917 addressed his second message, delivered just after coming to power, to the "Toiling Muslims of Russia and East." So they considered Muslims a reservoir of people for the world communist revolution.

Lynne Stewart, who represented the "blind sheik," terrorist cleric Omar Abdel-Rahman, had told the Marxist *Monthly Review* magazine that radical Islamists are "basically forces of national liberation." She was referring to Islamists taking down the Egyptian government but we have seen that the threat to Europe is very real indeed.

Understanding Marxist dialectics is absolutely critical to unraveling and understanding the history of the Russian use of Islamic and Arab terrorist groups.

The old Soviet Union always sought to divide the U.S. from Germany and its other allies in NATO and Europe. The Soviet-supported international terrorist networks that included such groups as the Red Army Faction in then-West Germany were part of this campaign. The Islamists we face today learned their style of warfare from the Soviets, who established the Palestine Liberation Organization (PLO) as the pivot point for the Soviet Union's strategic approach to world revolution, especially control of the Middle East. PLO chief Yasser Arafat was a KGB agent, while al-Qaeda leader Ayman al-Zawahiri was trained by the Soviet intelligence service.

Strategic analyst Michael Ledeen has concluded, in regard to the activities of the Islamic State, "I think the Russians are involved, in tandem with the Iranians, who have had their own troops on the Syrian battlefield for years." He said, "It's part of the global war, of which Syria is only one killing field, and IS [Islamic State] is one of the band of killers."

The analysis of Ledeen, who previously served as a consultant to the National Security Council, the State Department, and the Defense Department, should serve as an opportunity to review what is really happening in the Middle East, and to examine whether the Islamic State is a Russian creation that is designed to pave the way for Iranian expansion.[30]

Ledeen notes evidence that the top IS military commander, Abu Omar al-Shishani, is a Russian asset, and that "the Russians are exploiting their strategic position in Ukraine to set up transit facilities for IS." He adds that Ukrainian security forces recently arrested five IS volunteers coming from Russia or the former Soviet republics.

Indeed, we have heard repeatedly about Americans and Europeans fighting for ISIL, but little attention is being devoted to the Russian-speaking foreign fighters that make up the group. Their numbers are estimated at 500 or more. Omar al-Shishani is usually described as a prominent Islamic State fighter who is Chechen. In fact, he was born in the former Soviet republic of Georgia and was trained there.

Marius Laurinavičius, Senior Policy Analyst in the Policy Analysis and Research Division of the Eastern Europe Studies Center, argues in his paper, "Do traces of KGB, FSB and GRU lead to Islamic State?," that it is impossible to understand the rise of the Islamic state without paying attention to the links between the Russian secret services and Arab/Muslim terrorists, including in the Russian region of Chechnya. The Islamic terrorism that is targeting Europe and the U.S. is literally "made in Moscow."

The U.S. war against ISIL has led to what the *Wall Street Journal* called in a July 25, 2015, sensational story "America's New Marxist Allies." The story noted that the Kurdistan Workers' Party, or PKK, a "cultlike Marxist-inspired group," had "emerged as Washington's most effective battlefield partners against Islamic State, also known as ISIS, even though the U.S. and its allies have for decades listed the PKK as a terrorist group."

Hence, a defeat of the Russian-backed Islamic State could benefit another communist-linked group. In either case, enemies of Western-style democracy and capitalism emerge as winners.

In another area of global affairs that reveals a hidden Russian role, *The New York Times* has taken note in a June 7, 2015 story of evidence that the Russians under Putin are financing conservative movements and political parties around the world. The Times reports, "Not only is it [the Kremlin] aligning itself with the leftists traditionally affiliated with Moscow since the Cold War, but it is making common cause with far-right forces rebelling against the rise of the European Union that are sympathetic to Mr. Putin's attack on what he calls the West's moral decline."

This is actually an old story. We have been reporting for years and in our book on Russia about Putin acquiring agents of influence or dupes in the West, even in the United States. Perhaps the most prominent name associated with this pro-Moscow trend is veteran conservative columnist Patrick J. Buchanan. The World Congress of Families is the most prominent organization to embrace Moscow's alleged devotion to Christian values.

It is a welcome development that *The New York Times* finally took notice of Moscow's hand in right-wing political movements. But there's more. The paper added, "American and European officials have accused Moscow of financing green movements in Europe to encourage protests against hydraulic fracturing, or fracking, a move intended to defend Russia's gas industry."

The battle for Europe is also economic and political. The late anti-communist analyst Christopher Story's book, *The European Union Collective: Enemy of its Member States,* examined German and Russian designs for dominance of Europe. Our book, *Back from the Dead: Return of the Evil Empire,* cites evidence that German Chancellor Angela Merkel is an agent of influence for Russia's Vladimir Putin.[31]

Analyst J.R. Nyquist notes that Merkel was known to be suspiciously pro-Russian when she ran for high office in Germany but that her political party, the Christian Democrats, nominated her anyway, "and now Germany is more dependent on Russian natural gas than ever before." Germany's so-called "unique relationship with Russia" means that the country gets

36 percent of its natural gas imports and 39 percent of its oil imports from Russia.

The increasing dependence on Russia is related to Merkel's decision, after the accident at the Fukushima nuclear plant in Japan, to phase out Germany's nuclear energy program. Pressure to cancel Germany's nuclear program had come from the German Green Party.

A prominent member of the German Green Party, Hans-Christian Ströebele, met with NSA leaker Edward Snowden in Moscow and gave him a "whistleblower" award. He previously served as a lawyer for the Soviet- and East German-backed terrorist group, the Red Army Faction (also known as the Baader Meinhof Gang), and was sentenced to 10 months imprisonment in 1982 for setting up a communications network between the terrorist prisoners and activists outside the jails.

Professor Steven Alan Samson of Liberty University notes that "...the Soviet empire began collapsing just as the Left managed to hijack the European project..." Vladimir Bukovsky and Pavel Stroilov, the authors of *EUSSR*, characterize the plan as an example of the Marxist dialectic, in which conflict appeared to be a defeat for the Soviet Union but gave rise to another level of global integration in Europe subject to manipulation by Moscow and its agents.

We have seen this unfold in Greece, where a regime run by Alexis Tsipras, the pro-Marxist and pro-Russia head of Greece's "Coalition of the Radical Left," was bailed out by the European Union (EU), under Merkel's direction. Tsipras's political party, Syriza, is a member of The European Left, whose member parties are described as "socialist, communist, red-green and other democratic left parties of the member states and associated states of the European Union." Tsipras, vice president of the European Left, had met with Putin in Moscow.

Hence, through the bailout of Greece, the EU is in effect financing a form of Russian expansion and infiltration of Europe and the EU. This begins to fulfill the vision of Mikhail Gorbachev, author of *Perestroika*, who referred to the "Common European Home." He meant by that Soviet or Russian domination of Europe.

The Communist Conquest of Africa

The Monroe Doctrine was supposed to protect U.S. national security interests in the Western hemisphere by prohibiting foreign meddling in America's backyard. Vladimir Putin seems to share Secretary of State John Kerry's belief that this national security doctrine is dead. Putin traveled to Brazil, Argentina, Nicaragua and Cuba in 2014. Russia is talking about establishing new military bases in Cuba, Venezuela and Nicaragua. China policy expert Richard Fisher says Chinese activities in the Western hemisphere, include nine canal programs and ten port and airport programs throughout Latin America. Yet, anti-American regimes are also in place in Africa and working with Russia and China.

The "Free World" considers South Africa to be free, despite the fact that longtime leader Nelson Mandela concealed his membership in the South African Communist Party (SACP). In the book, *Mandela: The Authorized Biography*, Anthony Sampson writes that Mandela started out as an anti-communist but "was impressed by The Communist Manifesto and by the biographies of South African Marxists like Paul Bunting and Bill Andrews." Sampson said Mandela "was struck by the Soviet Union's support for liberation movements throughout the world, and by the relentless logic of dialectical materialism, which he felt sweeping away the superstitions and inherited beliefs of his childhood..." One of those beliefs was Christianity, and Sampson writes that Mandela "experienced some pangs at abandoning the Christian beliefs that had fortified his childhood…"

Like a true Marxist, Mandela concealed his membership in the SACP (until it was revealed after his death by the SACP and other sources) because the element of deception is absolutely necessary to fool the West. Southern Africa, with its strategic minerals, was a critical prize during the Cold War. Soviet leader Leonid I. Brezhnev had told Somalian President Siad Barre, "Our aim is to gain control of the two great treasure houses on which the West depends—the energy treasure house of the Persian Gulf and the mineral treasure house of Central and Southern Africa."

Today, South Africa is a member of the Russian-sponsored BRICS alliance of nations, and is actively pursuing nuclear deals with Russia. The regime of South African President Jacob Zuma, a "former" member of the Communist Party, has even developed a "strategic partner" relationship with the Russian government.

"The South African Road to Socialism," a document on the website of the South African Communist Party, covers the period from 2012 to 2017. The document talks about the "mobilization of private capital into an NDR [National Democratic Revolution]" and how "transforming" the capitalist market is essential to progress. It is the same path chosen by the communists in China and Russia.

Few people understand the dialectical process that is underway because the assumption is that communism has "collapsed" and capitalism has triumphed. Communists have always allowed for a form of capitalism, in order to strengthen the forces of socialism and communism.

At the memorial service for Mandela, the Marxist President of Zimbabwe, Robert Mugabe, received "thunderous applause."

Mugabe won power in April 1980, in a free parliamentary election, which Ian Smith, the white leader who had declared Southern Rhodesia's independence, and his moderate black allies had agreed to hold. The country was renamed Zimbabwe. Within five years, half the whites had fled the country, and the minority black tribes were as dissatisfied as the whites. Thousands of Mugabe's political opponents had been killed by his army. His rivals had been exiled or neutralized, and Mugabe had proclaimed his intention to establish a one-party state. The once-prosperous country was in serious economic trouble and had become dependent on foreign aid. Nearly a million people have fled to South Africa from Zimbabwe. But hundreds of thousands of whites left South Africa following Mandela's landslide election victory in 1994. In the years ahead, as the economy and race relations deteriorate, an exodus of more whites is expected.

Interview with Former Intelligence Official

Cliff Kincaid: Today we're talking with a former government employee and intelligence agency official, whom we will call the "Insider." He served many years abroad studying the topic of Marxist dialectical thought. We're going to get into this not only in its theoretical or philosophical dimensions, but in practical terms - what Marxist dialectics means and how it plays out in real life such as in the fundamental transformation of the United States as well as globally.

Now let's begin with a basic question: is international communism dead?

Insider: I think the easiest way to answer that would be to go to the Internet and ask Google how many communist parties are there in the world and you'd probably find that almost every country in the world has a Communist Party. What do the communist parties have? Together they have a common ideology that holds them together. They have meetings, they have international meetings, and it's very unlikely that they've given any of that up. It's the way in which they developed the struggle, because the conditions in the world have changed. But the idea that they have given up Marxism-Leninism is erroneous.

Cliff: Marxism-Leninism involves this dialectical notion of struggle that seems to be central to their ideology. What does that mean?

Insider: The Chinese wrote a lot of articles about it. Mao was a master at it. They wrote an article which called dialectic the algebra of revolution. Dialectics is a methodology and when you look at Marxism-Leninism they normally refer to it in two ways. One is dialectical materialism that tends to be the philosophical umbrella for all of Marxism. Generally you're looking at Marx, Engels and so on. But when they talk about the method they referred to it as materialist dialectic. It's a special kind of dialectics and it relates to the way in which one evaluates reality. It's more complex than that, but at least the way you look at reality and it means, basically, you're looking at it from a Marxist perspective. That means you are considering the way in which this methodology is used to communicate with each other and used to develop the revolutionary struggle around the world. It was fundamental to the Sino-Soviet polemic and it still is used. As a matter of fact, if you want to find out whether or not there is any commitment to it I would suggest simply going to the Constitution of the Communist Party of China and looking at about the first dozen paragraphs all committed to Marxism-Leninism and the revolution.

One of the things that is so fundamental to understanding Marxism Leninism is "struggle." Lenin said there's not a Marxist who doesn't probably believe this -- that without struggle there is no development. Why do we see chaos appearing in different places? Because, it is through struggle that development takes place, not through negotiations but through struggle. We have to disrupt things in order

73

to move it and in the United States for example we see a lot of these little organizations, things happening and so on, which are disruptive. They come probably from the left, a lot of them, simply because this disruption means that somebody has to take action. Somebody is involved in an activity that is in promotion of a particular point of view and it's going to be resisted by somebody. That resistance is another reason for activity. So wherever there is oppression there is resistance. When these organizations come up and talk about being oppressed, the idea is to promote resistance to it because, the resistance is disruptive and it means that somebody can do something about the disruption. Somebody is going to have to take action to quell it, to pacify it, so it's a way of moving things forward, struggle promotes development and there's no question about it. Can you see these damn things taking place, struggle promotes development and we keep getting it even though we don't want it

Dialectics is a scientific method and they call it science. It's the algebra of revolution which is pretty scientific. Absolutely. The dialectical methodology is a way of communicating with each other which is what they did through the Sino-Soviet polemic. The affirmation is passed through the negation. Now if you were sitting somewhere and you heard a couple Marxists talking, it wouldn't probably mean very much. The affirmation is passed through the negation. Basically what it means is, we say what we are for, by saying what we are against. This polemic was based pretty much on that, we say what we are for, by saying what we're against. When we criticize the Chinese, for example, we are saying, to everybody who doesn't understand dialectics, it's a criticism. And most all of us looking at that would see it as criticism and when we see criticism, we see two people who aren't in agreement. But, if underlying all of that, if in fact you have a way of saying when I criticize you, the opposite of what the criticism is, is what I am for. Therefore if I say, you are a splitter that means to us, that means he's not Orthodox. But the opposite would be orthodoxy and you make a case out of that for the orthodoxy so I would have a chance.

Cliff: Since you brought up China and the Sino-Soviet split, so-called, let's get into that. It's been commonly believed and said, stated as a fact, that Russia and China have basically abandoned communism. Do you believe this?

Insider: Of course not. I mean, as I just mentioned, if you go to the constitution of the Communist Party of China there is no way you can look at the opening paragraphs of the Constitution for the party and come to the conclusion that they have abandoned it. One paragraph after another affirms its fidelity to the principles of Marxism-Leninism and Mao Zedong thought. Also go to the internet and look up the words "Gennady Zyuganov." You will find out that Zyuganov and Putin are apparently fairly good friends, on good terms and associate with each other. As a matter of fact a year and a half or two ago, Putin asked Zyuganov, who is chairman of the Communist

Party of Russia, to speak. Even though there's no association of Putin to a Communist Party of Russia, the fact that he's president of Russia, certainly suggests that he has the ability to control the movement of almost any political party or political organization and he obviously accepts the Communist Party of Russia.

More than that, at one point as a former member of the KGB, he would have been a party member himself and had been appointed as head of the KGB by Boris Yeltsin and the party. I haven't read anything that suggests that he's given up any of that. The other factor in all of this is, there are two ways of evaluating Marxist reality. One is in theory and then the second way is practice. And for a Marxist no matter which party you come from the practice is the sole criterion of truth. If you want to find out whether or not they are really Marxist, you have to know what the Marxist theory is in a given situation and then you examine the social practices and revolutionary practices of the party to see whether or not they conform to the theory. If they do, then they are just right along where they should be.

Cliff: When you see countries like China or even Russia to some extent opening up their economies to certain free market forces, to some form of capitalism, doesn't that mean they've given up communism or Marxist Leninism?

Insider: That just means they've made adjustments. I've forgotten which Chinese leader, but one of them at one point some years ago said, "socialists don't have to be poor," or something to that effect. Of course, there's another great common term which is extremely useful I think in understanding Marxist dialectics, that's the term "conditions." Nothing happens favorably unless the conditions are there to have it happen. For example, man didn't go into space, why? Because the conditions weren't there. What do you have to do in order to put man in space? They have a phrase called "create conditions." So that you have to create the conditions to accomplish your goal. Now they want to have a prosperous society. There's nothing in Marxism that says you can't be prosperous. There's nothing that I remember. So China is trying to develop a prosperous social society. One of the benefits of a prosperous social society is the fact that you don't have a struggle between the masses and the government because the people support it.

Cliff: So these countries, Russia and China, have opened up their economies to certain free market forces -- Western investment -- in order to make themselves stronger but they are still on the road to world communism and ultimately still intend to destroy us?

Insider: In my opinion, yes. Look at social practice and revolutionary practice in China. I go back to their Constitution. Look at the Constitution and see the commitment they have to Marxism and yet look at what they're doing economically. One of the criticisms they had of the Soviet Union was that

Gorbachev made his changes in the wrong place. He made them political, consequently he brought down the old Soviet Union in the form in which it existed and he should have developed the economy. China took the economic road and look at what happened with China.

Cliff: Since you brought up Gorbachev, let's get into that. I'm going to quote from Gorbachev and from your perspective if you can interpret this for us because Gorbachev himself in this 1987 book *Perestroika* referred to Marxist-Leninist dialectics many times. And he said, I'm quoting here, that the works of Lenin and his ideals of socialism remain an inexhaustible source of dialectical creative thought, theoretical wealth and political sagacity. And then he went on in this book to site what he called dialectical maneuvers that Lenin had used. Therefore, was perestroika a dialectical maneuver designed to confuse us or mislead us about his real intentions and what they were trying to do?

Insider: I don't think it was so much to mislead us; he already knew that we're probably not going to understand it. Basically what this comes down to, if you don't have a really firm grounding in Marxism-Leninism and dialectical thought, whatever they do is going to be a mystery and they like to keep it a mystery. They are not anxious for us to understand it in the same way in which they do. As long as we misunderstand it we can't act correctly against it.

Cliff: Was the so-called Sino-Soviet split a deception?

Insider: Yes it was. ~~What it was is a unifying struggle based upon dialectical negation.~~ One of the factors is that all Communist Parties can't act in the same way. Dialectically, was it a real split or not? The dialectical answer to that would be it was, and yet it was not. ~~A lot of questions in dialectics are answered in that manner. Is this true? Yes, it is under certain conditions and under certain conditions it is not true.~~ Therefore yes it is true and yet it is not. In the Sino-Soviet polemic, what happened was that a united Marxist-Leninist component was facing a united defense against it. It was getting in the way of revolutionary development, creating a revolutionary obsession among people around the world. Therefore, how are we going to change this in our favor?

I think it came out of North Africa -- the idea was that there was a division between China and the Soviet Union. How did this develop? The smallest country in the Marxists world was Albania. So it came out that Albania and Russia were having a dispute. Well who would believe, at that time, that the little Albania would take on the Soviet Union? Nobody, but they have to test this theory so they put Albania and Russia in kind of a juxtaposition in terms of the dispute over some aspect of revolutionary development. We accepted that so what happened was it turned out, it came out that ~~Albania was a kind of a surrogate for China~~. That in fact, the real dispute was between China and the Soviet Union. And so we became willing to accept that. How did they develop that struggle, through a series of dialectical negations. China would accuse Russia of some error in Marxist development and that gave the Russians an opportunity to negate that negation. So Russia would accuse China of some false step and that gave China an opportunity to negate that negation.

There's a very good book called *The Polemic.* When you look at that there's a series of articles that are compiled, this was put out by the Chinese, a series of articles that go back and forth in terms of criticism of each other. When you read the criticism, for example, the criticism by China of the Soviet Union, you find out when you try to verify that criticism it doesn't exist. You'll find criticism from a document from the Communist Party of Russia about China and when you try to verify that criticism, you find out it doesn't exist. But for us, what did we see in that? A series of arguments which we really didn't understand but which seem to us to indicate there were serious differences between the two. Were there serious differences? Of course, you've got two people on the same path with a discussion about how should we best approach our ultimate goal, which was world socialism, world communism. So there are bound to be differences. And what they did is they played those differences up. And each difference gave the Soviet criticism of China, gave China a chance to negate a negation from the Soviet Union. And whether the Soviet Union negated something that China did or they didn't like, it gave China a chance to rebut that. So they were playing a game all the time in terms of mutual negations and the negations are there to developed the whole program.

Cliff: So yet they are still united in the sense that they're both on the road to World Communism?

Insider: Sure.

Cliff: When we see the criticism between the Russians and the Chinese, the Communist Parties criticizing each other, we think they're not in agreement.

Insider: That's what we think.

Cliff: But you're saying that they are in agreement, this is just really an argument among friends.

Insider: Absolutely. Let me give you another example. Deng Xiaoping was making a speech at the Great Hall of the People, and he invited all of diplomats and so on, the Soviet ambassador, members of his staff, communist bloc ambassadors, members of their staff. And a little way into the speech, Deng Xiaoping criticizes the Soviet Union; let's say that he called them "splitters." This is a negation of the Soviet Union's theoretical orthodoxy. Now the Soviets have an obligation to do two things. One is to either accept that criticism or to reject it. And as a good Marxist of course you are going to reject it. So how can one, how can they reject that criticism? They can leave it where it is, which basically they did from our point of view, and they did that by walking out.

When Deng Xiaoping leveled that criticism the Soviet ambassador and his staff got up and walked out along with some of the other bloc ambassadors. We saw that as absolute proof, of the fact, that there is a split between these two. Now the Soviet ambassador could've done that and left it up to Moscow to comment to Beijing, you can't say that about us. But in fact it's a form of negation. Getting up and walking out is a form of negation. The ambassador is saying, we disagree with you, we're Orthodox, we reject what you say. Well if we reject what you say, that means we believe in something else. What do we believe in? We say we are a Communist Party. There's a Communist Party and we're Communist Party members and we're members of the Communist Party of Russia, we're walking out, we reject what you say. So the negation was to walk out.

We saw it as a conflict but in fact from a Marxist perspective it is simply a negation of Deng Xiaoping's negation. It's kind of complex and unless you really understand dialectics, it may not make a lot of sense but dialectically it does

Cliff: It's a whole different mindset.

Insider: Absolutely. Criticism and self-criticism are fundamental to the Communist Party and in the Communist Party. The idea is not to destroy the one you're criticizing. Criticism is to promote a better relationship. The criticism of China over the Soviet Union and vice versa was not to destroy socialism. Let's say China criticizes the Soviet Union for something or other, it's not to destroy the Communist Party or the Soviet Union but to improve the conditions and vice versa. Why do you criticize a communist party member? It is to improve him in making him a better communist. The idea of self-criticism is that a man views himself as a communist and asks, "What are my errors? What can I do to make myself a better communist?" When they did it internationally, one party to another party, the idea is when we criticize you, here's what we perceive to be in error or mistake. It gives you an opportunity to improve the situation and change and improve yourself as a Communist Party.

Cliff: But they're still comrades.

Insider: Of course. Because the idea is not the destruction of one or the other, it's the improvement of one or the other.

Now, getting back to "perestroika" in that book. Gorbachev concludes the book by saying "we are moving toward a new world, the world of communism we shall never turn off that road."

Cliff: So what was "perestroika" then in their estimation? What did it do for them or to us in terms of Russia continuing on the road to World Communism? What was it designed to accomplish?

Insider: Well it was designed to accomplish a reorganization within the Soviet Union, in order to strengthen the position of the party and position within the World Communist Movement. The problem was, as I just mentioned a while ago was, that he chose the wrong place to organize. He chose political organization over economic reorganization. This criticism comes from the Chinese who said that he should have reorganized economically.

Cliff: So Gorbachev did make a mistake? And that mistake resulted in the demise of the old USSR?

Insider: And the breakup of the Soviet bloc.

Cliff: That was real?

Insider: That was real.

Cliff: But since then, they realized their error and they have been trying to reconstitute the old Soviet Union. Is this what Putin is trying to do?

Insider: I don't think they have so much a desire to reorganize the Soviet Union as the old Soviet Union but creating a federation of states which have a common unity. If they can bring the Baltic states and Ukraine back in some form of political union, they'll create a Federation and what will come out of that of course will be each will have a communist party. I don't think they're anxious to do that simply because it's going to create an obstacle from their point of view, which would be our resistance.

Cliff: But has there been any resistance?

Insider: Not very effective

Cliff: Let me ask you about another important country in the world today, South Africa. Mandela has been exposed as a secret communist and South Africa is a member of the BRICS alliance of nations. Like the U.S., South Africa has gone through a radical transformation. What does that mean in Marxist terms?

Insider: Let's just deal with transformation without the radical part. In dialectical thought, everything is divided into two. Everything divides into two. Every concept, every idea, every term and so on is divided into two opposites. The opposites are in conflict with each other. And for example, if you take this society, an example of a division into two would be proletariat and bourgeoisie. And from a Marxist perspective what is the goal of a Marxist perspective? A Marxist party, it's a capitalist society. Transformation of what? Of the capitalist society into a socialist society ultimately to a communist society which is way down the road.

So we might take two opposites within the framework of a capitalist society, what are the two leading classes? Bourgeoisie and proletariat. Those are called aspects and each aspect determines what direction something's taking. The leading aspect is the one that dominates the society. In a capitalist society the dominate aspect is the bourgeoisie. So when you look at America and Europe, some of the European societies, it's dominated by the bourgeoisie. And what

85

is the goal of the proletariat? To overthrow the bourgeoisie and transform the bourgeoisie into the proletarian state. "Transform" is a fundamental term and every time you hear it, transform, it means changing one thing into its opposite and so you hear it even in our country we're transformed. It's not well defined because the people using it don't tell us what it is they desire to transform. But if you are a Marxist, I would say in the United States, you already know. You don't have to be told. Because you're a Marxist and you know what it's supposed to be so you don't have to be told what it is. But this idea is the same we transform the society from one kind of society to another. We transform one class into another class. We transform the bourgeoisie into the proletariat. The proletariat becomes the leading aspect. They dominate the society and the Communist Party is the vanguard of the proletariat.

Cliff: Now in the United States though we have various Communist parties. We have the old Moscow-controlled and funded Communist Party but we have others like the Workers World Party. I can go down a list of these. Which one is the most important? Or, are they all working together and are they all under foreign influence? How would you assess that?

Insider: Look at the one that has the most dominance in the world. I would say the Communist Party of the United States. It's the biggest, best-funded, the best trained and all the other smaller ones are just little factions that are helping in effect the Communist

Party of the United States because they're all going in the same direction. They just go about it a little differently. It's somewhat like the international communist movement. Not every party can develop and every country in the same fashion. Each has to depend upon the conditions. So they create some of these smaller Communist parties which come in and say "we don't like the way the Communist Party in the United States is developing a struggle, we should do it this way." They're both developing the struggle. The only question is which way they want to go, so that the little party makes its contribution by being an annoyance over here, another one is an annoyance over here, but fundamentally when the chips are really down, the Communist Party in the United States, which is the biggest, the best-funded and has the most international context, and is looked at by the major communist parties, is going to be dominant.

Cliff: When we look at these terms that have a Marxist significance like transformation another one comes to mind this term "the people." What Marxist significance in dialectical terms does that have?

Insider: That's kind of an easy one. Lenin I think wrote an essay a long time ago on who were the people. Simply defined, the people are those who support the revolution and those who oppose the revolution are the enemies of the people. The people are those who support the revolution. So you have to be careful when you see government leaders around the world, especially left wing government leaders, using the term the people or speaking on behalf of the people. You're going to have to find some way to make sure you understand who they mean. Do they mean the general population? Let me give you an example. Nixon went to China in 1972, I believe, and he was greeted at the airport by Zhou Enlai. So Nixon makes a little speech; he says the American people send their greetings to the people of China. And now when Nixon said that who did he mean by the people? He meant all of the people of the United States, the general population. We're all one; we give our greetings to the people in China. Zhou Enlai, his answer was the people of China send their greetings to the people of the United States. Now as a Marxist what did he means? He meant people in the Marxist sense, that is the people of China, who are the revolutionaries, those who support the revolution in China and the revolutionary process, send their greetings to the people of the United States. Did he mean all of the people of the United States? No, he meant the people who support the revolution. He didn't mean to send his greetings to the enemies of the revolution, which would be the general population of the United States, many of whom would oppose Marxism-Leninism. It's a semantical game in so many way.

Cliff: What do you say to those who would argue that the leaders of China and Russia and other countries around the world really don't believe in this Marxism anymore? That they realize it doesn't work, that they have to go capitalist to save their economies and they retain the reference to the Communist Party and allow the Communist Parties to exist but they don't really believe there's anything there worthwhile in terms of practical politics.

Insider: I say they are deceiving themselves to start with. Basically there are two ways one goes about evaluating that statement. One is you look at their theoretical statements from the parties. What do they want to accomplish? What are their goals, what are their aspirations? Then you have to apply what they would apply themselves. What is the sole criterion of determining truth for a Communist Party, for a Marxist? You have to apply that to the theory that they're talking about. The sole criterion of truth is practice. Do they practice? Do they endeavor to practice what they say they want to accomplish? Do they try to accomplish it? Are they outside the bounds of Marxism-Leninism? When you look at China, let's start with that one because everybody thinks they are on a capitalist road. You'd have to look at their goals, their aspirations. Where do you go? Two places, one is the constitution of the government to see what their national aspirations are for themselves and the people. Then you go to the Communist Party and you see what those goals and aspirations are. Then you look to see whether or not the goals of the party are basically in support of the national aspirations. And then you got to the social practice to see whether the party actually undertakes activities which in fact support the party goals, which are in fact supporting national goals.

Cliff: So we conclude on the basis of that analysis that the Chinese Communists still believe in communism?

Insider: Yes.

Cliff: That means they are still on the road to world communism, and that what we've been doing for decades in terms of treating them as taking this capitalistic road and trading with them, aiding them, this has all been a destructive course for the United States?

Insider: Yes.

Cliff: We are building up our enemy.

Insider: That's what we're good at.

Cliff: And we're doing the same with Russia?

Insider: Absolutely.

Cliff: You've argued that Vladimir Putin is still a communist. He's certainly a "former" KGB colonel. We have built them up after the "demise of the old Soviet Union" and yet they're still dedicated to destroying us?

Insider: Absolutely. There's no particular set path for doing that because in a sense they've never been successful yet, but I think that is an interesting point because what you get into are forms of struggle. And it is a very common phrase. Marxism teaches, especially Mao, that you must apply all forms of struggle against the enemy. What is a form of struggle? Anything that attacks the enemy is a form of struggle. It can take place in the workplace, it can take place in a factory, it can take place in the union, it can take place anywhere but anything which works to change, transform a part of the society in a way which is favorable to the Marxists, is a form of struggle.

So when you look at some of the materials you mentioned, some of these Communist Party materials, and you read the newspapers and so on, you see what they attack. One of the things that is fundamental to any form of struggle is you always attack the main enemy.

Why do they attack such people as the Koch brothers? I don't know anything about the Koch brothers, other than the name. The Marxist looks at people like that and they see people standing in their way and you have got to destroy those who have the most influence in preventing you from doing what you do. So they'll use anything they can, they'll attack his personality, attack his background, there are a lot of different ways.

Cliff: Even though the Koch brothers are big businessmen who do business with China and Russia?

Insider: Sure.

Cliff: So they are picked on just because they are a symbol? Is that what that attack is meant to serve?

Insider: They'll use them at the same time you have to attack them. So we find that people attack them for the influence that they exert in preventing the movement from going ahead. At the same time they'll exploit the Koch brothers, if the Koch brothers or people like that are able to put resources to use in some area which the party can use. It's a matter of making distinctions all the way along the line. It's not a permanent structure against them. It's how do we exploit them? When they get in our way we attack them. Where they help us we defend them. We use them. It's a really artful way of developing a revolution.

Cliff: When we look at what's happening internationally, as well as domestically in the United States, how do we educate the American people about what is really happening, how our enemies are still active and deceiving us, deceiving our government leaders, our policy makers? How do we get a handle on this enemy which regards us as their main enemy?

Insider: Marxists have a way of getting their message across and I'm sure you are very familiar with front organizations. So you have interlocking front organizations, all of whom are presenting certain points of view around throughout the country and as a means of getting their message out. I think without a corresponding set of front organizations which present democracy as we are all accustomed to thinking about it, desiring to have it, it's very difficult. Even the American Legion can get a message out which is contrary to the Marxist message. But we don't have any kind of systematic approach or focal point. The Communist Party of the United States has a message. All of the Communist parties, even little organized ones that are not thought of in any serious way, know what that message is. They're all Marxists, they all believe in the ultimate goal; they just don't believe we can all get there the same way. But, the fact that they're putting out a common message enhances the one single common message for all of them. They're so better organized than we are. Organization is really a key for them and they've been at it for seventy, eighty years. They know what the hell they're doing. They know how to do it and we have yet to catch up

Cliff: Mao said, "Great disorder across the land leads to great order." What did he mean?

Insider: Great disorder means great reorganization. The greater the upheaval or the greater the disorder and the greater the opportunity for reorganization. If things seem to be sort of becoming unglued in places, keep in mind that somebody is going to glue it together. It's going to be glued together perhaps in a way that we are not really very happy. So if somebody is doing, undertaking ideas that many of the people of the United States, that people don't really like, that is going to create some upheaval, some resistance and that resistance has to be dealt with and who is going to deal with it?

Cliff: This is part of the struggle?

Insider: Yes. In other words, you want to create disorder because you want to be able to reorganize. So the more disorder you can create within the framework of society the more opportunity you have to intervene and create that. Passivity doesn't get you very far because everything remains the same. You don't advance very far but creating disorder advances a lot of things in a way even though it's in a way we don't like because it gives an opportunity for people who are well-organized, who are leading the disorder, to get in involved and to recreate the society in a way in which they want it. To transform it in a way in which they want it.

Cliff: Those of us who are conservative people, we want to maintain the stability of our society, our families, our country, the world and we are seeing things coming unglued. More disorder, more chaos. But you're saying this is a plan.

Insider: Yes.

Cliff: So this is designed to undermine everything we hold dear so that as it comes unglued the representatives of "the people" will then transform society into this revolutionary situation.

Insider: The question is: are there people who would destroy our society and transform it into something which most of us don't want? Absolutely. Are they active? Absolutely. Do we know who they are? I'm sure the FBI does and a whole lot of other people and people in your organization and other organizations know who these people are, who would transform the United States from a capitalist society to a socialist society. Once it's a socialist society, what is the next transformation? Ultimately communism. Who is going to do the transformation of the society from socialism to communism? The Communist Party, which is the vanguard of all revolutionary elements. Consequently the idea of creating disorder is an opportunity for the intervention of the Communist Party and for communists to get involved. Where? In unions, in social activities and social organizations.

The left in our country is extremely well organized. They know what the techniques are and the values are, how to infiltrate, where to infiltrate. I read somewhere, a long time ago, that our Congress contains 60 or so communists or socialists. Deception comes in politically when a socialist runs as a Democrat and tells the American people, "I'm a Democrat like you are," when in fact he's a socialist. These people come in and their loyalty is where? They take the oath of office to the United States of America, when in fact their fundamental loyalty is to the socialist cause. My question is, where is their fundamental loyalty? Is it to the Democratic Party, which we think of as a democratic organization historically in a way with which most of us can accept? Or is their loyalty to the socialist cause, acting through the Democratic Party?

Cliff: How extensive is the use of these useful idiots or dupes?

Insider: They can't do without them. They exist everywhere. I mean, I would say that a lot of the people in Congress are useful idiots. I mean that when you think about who's ultimately going to win, that's a fundamental question. To me it's going be the Marxists if the struggle goes far enough and we don't get a hold of it. A lot of our Congress people probably find it very useful to be on the side of the left because the left identifies them, promotes them, helps them along and maybe gives financial contribution. But when the chips are down and the party has to make a decision, whether this person is somebody they really want they are going to find they're really nobody. I mean you think of somebody like Al Sharpton and so on he won't be anybody of any importance to the Marxist movement. He may think he is now because he is useful to them. But he isn't going to be within the framework of the Communist Party-dominated governmental leadership, he won't be anybody. There will be a lot of others coming up who have proven their worth and value through the system by being members and working on behalf of the party in an organized way in a knowledgeable way.

Cliff: What about the role of Muslims. How would you assess that? Are they pawns of the Communist movement? Are they being used against us? Do they pose any threat to the communist movement? How do you see that?

Insider: I would say that they're a threat to the communists. After all, a communist is as much of an infidel as we are. And I don't see where the two can come together. As a matter of fact it seems to me that what the world is really waiting for is for the Muslims to try to infiltrate China and Russia and probably get their heads hammered, because there is no way in the world that I think that they are going to be able to take over and dominate. Russia and China can be vicious when it comes to that sort of thing and I don't think they're going to accept any kind of movement by Islam into their countries. Chechnya is already a good example of the way the Russians are willing to treat them.

Cliff: At the same time, looking at the history of Soviet support for international terrorism and groups like the PLO, the Palestine Liberation Organization, various Marxist Islamic or Palestinian groups, doesn't it appear that while these countries China and Russia may perceive Islam to be an ultimate threat to them, that they can use the threat against us?

Insider: Absolutely. To them it's another form of struggle. Any place where you can put the West in jeopardy and force the West to focus its attention in essence somewhere else you just do it. Sure, they use these organizations all the time. Islamists will believe that when they cooperate with the Soviets and Chinese or any Marxist revolutionary organization that they're helping themselves. And the Marxist organization believes they're helping themselves. The question is who is really helping whom? In the given conditions for a short period of time one may be right and the other may be wrong. One may benefit really but, then as condition changes, as they inevitably will or the way they relate to each other, will also change. So in these conditions they can say we're going to work together but as a year goes by, conditions have changed, and all of a sudden now they no longer can find that they can cooperate on that basis. They have to seek either a new basis for cooperation or come to some other arrangements strategically or tactically.

Understanding Marxist Dialectics

By "The Insider"

It is evident that those who know the strategy of one kind of game can often apply its general principles to games of a similar character, and it is equally evident that to learn to play an unfamiliar game well one needs to study its rules, strategy and tactics. On the surface there is nothing very profound about such an observation. People throughout the world play a variety of games, and take for granted that one who wishes to play will need to understand the fundamental principles and rules which underlie them. We can assume, given the objective and subjective resources, that those so armed can both compete in a game and even expect to win it.

In man's more normal pursuits few, if any, would knowingly enter into a game or contest without foreknowledge of how it is to be played, since victory would be uncertain at best, and it would not likely be fun for those involved. However, this construction applies to games in which one is a willing competitor and participant.

Obviously, many games are played in which an individual may have no interest and the matter of the game's strategy and rules is then unimportant to him. Games that are lengthy, inordinately involved, costly in terms of time and equipment needed, require study, or which for one reason or another, one simply does not desire to play, are similarly unimportant to a

99

person. In most societies and for most people that would be the end of the matter. People are not normally involved in games they do not wish to play.

However, there are yet other kinds of games which people play either individually or collectively which often involve one or more people unwillingly and/or unwittingly. The normal tendency for those unwillingly embroiled in games organized, led, and played by others, is to fight against such complicity, ignore the game, and pretend that because one is unwilling to play he is then uninvolved. Those participating in games unwittingly are simply passive pawns who are moved, directed and manipulated by forces of which they are not even aware.

If then, one adds complicated rules to such a game, rules which the instigator deliberately makes obscure, hiding them in many different places requiring extensive research to learn them, then, under these conditions, an individual would find it almost impossible to play the game even if he should desire to do so.

The foregoing is analogous to the present political situation in which many people find themselves today. The game is a world "struggle" to determine which way of life is superior. It is principally developed by those supporting a political and economic philosophy demanding of them that they undertake; a variety of methods and struggle to prove the supremacy of this ideology. In this game of world politics the rules have been drawn up by Marx,

Engels, and Lenin, and further developed by the various "philosophers" of the Soviet Union, China, as well as the other socialist countries supporting the same worldview.

The "rules" they have developed for this game are couched in dialectical language, virtually foreign to those who do not understand it as do its proponents, and the definitions and keys are hidden in the many writings of various communists, most notably Lenin and Mao Zedong. Equally hidden are the rules which tell how the dialectical language and method is to be used in a practical way to achieve their "historical mission."

All communists since Marx, Engels and Lenin have accepted dialectics as their best analytical tool to interpret world events, and as a "sharp weapon" to change the world. They have repeated in a variety of ways Lenin's comment that dialectics is the "living soul" of Marxism. Lin Biao, once heir apparent to Mao Zedong, called dialectics a "spiritual atom bomb," far superior to the real thing.

In spite of the communist emphasis upon the need for revolutionaries to learn the dialectical method, Western scholars have largely ignored it. For example, Mao Zedong's basic writings still have not been dealt with seriously in the West. Yet the proper study of these works could help one to understand many communist actions which otherwise are considered incomprehensible; e.g., the role of the Sino-Soviet polemic in advancing the revolutionary struggle; the meaning of otherwise puzzling slogans such as "unity in diversity;" "dare to go against the tide;" or how the Chinese dialectical attacks on the CPSU actually strengthens the CPSU and the communist movement. For the communists an understanding of the "dialectical method" is the only method to understand their world outlook and reality.

For example, the principle of one divides into two is the "most correct expression of dialectics," and it can be shown with absolute precision that communists employ this method in resolving their conflicts and contradictions. Yet, virtually no one in the West outside Marxist-Leninist organizations has studied, explored, or explained the use of dialectics as a practical revolutionary weapon.

More importantly, neither has it been explained how the communists actually apply the method in their revolutionary practice. In spite of differences between the Chinese and Soviets it can be shown through communist texts that the Chinese and Soviets are working to resolve "non-antagonistic" contradictions between themselves, and to prevent them from becoming "antagonistic." Their "fights," "squabbles," "polemics," however they may be characterized, are a natural consequence of their system and world outlook, accepted by them and dealt with through a universally accepted method known as "criticism and self-criticism." They consider this to be the only commonly accepted method to resolve differences among communists and communist parties. It is, for them, a "scientific method."

Most importantly, there is unity among the principal communist parties in the world socialist system as to what constitutes the rules and laws of dialectics; they all profess the same things and understand the concepts in the same way. All are in agreement with Lenin, for example, who said that the central problem and "nucleus" of dialectics was the problem of contradiction. The Soviets have summarized the core of dialectics as a "division into opposites" while Mao Zedong and the Chinese "workers of philosophy" have finally summarized all the complexities of dialectical logic into the expression "one divides into two." In essence, there is no fundamental difference between the Soviet theoreticians and those in China as to what each of these expressions means.

On the other side, however, there are many Western scholars and analysts who contend that the dialectical approach is not "scientific," and, therefore, it is unworthy of study. But in reality, this objection means very little. Is the arbitrary value which is assigned to chess pieces "scientific?" Are the rules of a soccer game or the points assigned to the scoring "scientific?" It would not seem so, but, in fact, they are useful since they determine how the games are to be played. Dialectics too is a game of sorts designed to win a worldwide historically inspired revolutionary victory for a presumed superior political and economic system. However, the real question is not the "scientific" nature of the rules and methods of dialectics, but do the rules and principles which the method's proponents have assigned to the game help them to play that game more efficiently, and can they indeed accomplish the goals to which they are dedicated. If Western analysts continue to ignore dialectics because they consider it unscientific, then that ignorance only serves to increase the method's effectiveness, but, more importantly, may also lead to serious miscalculations and consequences for all of mankind.

The Communist philosophers are, or course, well aware of Western ignorance of the dialectical method, and, certainly, do little to either encourage our study or to provide any kind of a textbook or "operator's manual" which will serve to guide our study. That such a study is badly needed in the present times is an understatement. If Western diplomats, politicians, government and others involved with the socialist countries indeed wish to develop coherent policies and strategies which will insure a correct understanding of the policies of the socialist countries, it can only be done with dialectics.

Given the opportunities for serious error to arise through Western ignorance of communist methodology, and the tragic consequences which might ensue -- a nuclear war, for example -- it is indeed vital to Western policy makers that they understand Marxist-Leninist dialectics in order to insure that no cataclysmic event can take place which would have tragic consequences for all mankind.

The Communist World Outlook

By "The Insider"

Is there such a thing as a communist world outlook?
If so, how did it come about and what is its content?
At the 24th Congress of the Communist Party of the
Soviet Union the following statement was made:

> The formation of a communist world outlook
> in the broad mass of the people and their
> education in the spirit of the ideas of
> Marxism-Leninism are the core of all
> ideological and educational work by the party.

Walter Lambrez, SED (Socialist Unity Party of
Germany) Politburo member, stated in a 1974 article
that "The Marxist-Leninist world outlook is . . . . a
total system of insights and convictions . . ."
Lambrez went on to say that the Marxist-Leninist
world outlook is not "contemplative but active" and
added, "It is therefore of overall social importance
that the question of ideology and world outlook are
increasingly being moved to the center of party
affairs."

In his 1937 essay *On Contradiction* Mao Zedong
said:

> Throughout the history of human knowledge,
> there have been two conceptions concerning
> the law of development of the universe, the
> metaphysical conception and the dialectical

conception, which form two opposing world outlooks.

All Marxist-Leninist parties subscribe to the same view without exception. It is this common world outlook which guide all Marxist-Leninist parties and which provides the ideological cement binding them together in pursuit of their common revolutionary aspirations.

If Communists agree that they have a shared world outlook, so too are they in agreement that those who oppose them in their scientific ideology and revolutionary objectives share a common world outlook, and it is on this basis that these two world outlooks "oppose each other." It can be said immediately that if the communists regard a world outlook to be the means whereby one cognized reality and then acts on the basis of that cognition; that if for them there are two opposing world outlooks then the same facts and the world will have quite a different meaning for each. For example, Mao Zedong says in his essay, "A single Spark Can Start a Prairie Fire", that appearance and essence are not the same thing, that appearance is only an usher at the threshold of the essence of a thing. He further states that appearance may in fact distort reality. Thus we should be cautioned from accepting what seems to be true as either the whole truth or even the accurate reflections of truth - - it may be true and yet it may not. The Sino-Soviet polemic which began in the early 1960's has had a profound effect on the foreign policies of non-communist countries since they have taken the appearance of great division between the two communist giants, the USSR and the People's Republic of China, to be exactly what it appears to be and to conclude there are no unifying aspects between the two. What are the facts? Utilizing the communist world outlook the answer is that the relationships between the Soviets and the Chinese combine both factors of unity and division in a special way, a "dialectical way", and the appearance does not conform with the essence - - in fact, the appearance of the Sino-Soviet polemic as perceived by most Western analysts actually distorts the essence of that polemic. It is not seen by high-level Marxist-Leninists in the same way as it is by non-Marxist-Leninists. In partial confirmation of the foregoing assertion, Soviet Professor, M. Baglay, said in the January 9, 1975 edition of TRVD magazine: "It must be said that many people in the West have the wrong idea about our ideology and this is not surprising because for decades people have been living under a colossal press of misinformation and distortion of our life. In consequence of this many people still do not realize . . . the ideology of Communism." There is then a philosophy of communism with a main center where all threads of the world ideological and political struggle converge, and it is called by them the world socialists system - - a system upon which all contingents of the world revolutionary process depend.

What are these two world outlooks, their similarities and dissimilarities, and what is required for the correct understanding of Marxist-Leninist doctrine?

Mao Zedong in On *Contradiction* gives an excellent summary of the two world outlooks and it serves as the basic work for this discussion.

Mao states that the metaphysical or idealist outlook, called husuan-hsueh in Chinese, has occupied a dominant position in human thought for a long historical period, and even European materialism was metaphysical in its essence and remained the people's principal world outlook until the industrial proletariat became the greatest motive force in historical development. From this there arose the Marxist world outlook of materialist dialectics.

Marxist-Leninists contend those holding the metaphysical viewpoint see things in isolation, statically and one-sided. They see the forms and species of things in the universal as eternally separated from one another and immutable. Thus, if a thing changes, the nature of the change is only perceived as an increase or decrease in quantity or a change of place. The metaphysical viewpoint further believes that the motive cause of change in species or things is external to them, and that all the different kinds of things in the universe and all their characteristics have been the same ever since they came into being. As a consequence, changes are seen as simple increases or decreases in quantity, and a thing can only repeat itself as the same kind of thing and cannot change into or become a different thing. Mao further states that since metaphysicians believe that change results from development outside a thing they are, therefore, unable to explain in the qualitative diversity of things, nor the phenomenon of one quality changing into another. Mao cited an example of metaphysical thinking in China in the saying "Heaven changeth not, likewise the Tao changeth not." In Europe, Mao stated, such thinking was called mechanical materialism and vulgar evolutionism. He further amplified this view in 1955 when he said:

> The most economical theory in the world is idealism or metaphysics because it enables people to say whatever they wish, regardless of objective reality, with no need for corroboration with facts. Materialism and dialectics require hard work, as they have to rest on objective reality and be corroborated with facts. To save labor is to slip into idealism and metaphysics.

It is clear Mao does not regard "metaphysical" thinking highly nor the method which it imposes upon the user. With this brief description of the metaphysical outlook he sets the stage for a comparison of its opposite, the dialectical world outlook.

First, what is the value of the dialectical outlook? Mao summarized its value as follows: "This dialectical world outlook teaches us primarily how to observe and analyze the movement of opposites in different things and, on the basis of such analysis to indicate the methods for resolving contradictions in things."

Mao acknowledged that the dialectical outlook emerged in ancient times in both Europe and China. He stated that ancient dialectics were spontaneous and naïve in character and were still an unformed theoretical system incapable of fully explaining the world. Due to its insufficiencies it was supplanted for a time by another system, metaphysics, which dominated until the time of Hegel who made a most important contribution to the science of dialectics. Thus, while acknowledging Hegel's impact Mao also rejected the idealist nature and character of Hegel's work. "It was not until Marx and Engels... critically absorbed the rational elements of Hegelian dialectics and created the great theory of dialectical and historical materialism that an unprecedented revolution occurred in the history of human knowledge." This theory was further developed by Lenin and Stalin.

What then is the essence of the dialectical outlook and viewpoint? Mao states that "...the world outlook of materialist dialectics holds that in order to understand the development of a thing we should study it internally and in its relations to other things..." He added that development in things is caused by their internal, self-movement, yet, each thing is at the same time interrelated and interacting with things around it. Thus, even though things are externally related to and interacting with other things, "The fundamental cause of a development of a thing is not external but internal; it lies in the contradictoriness within the thing." With this assertion Mao stated what is basic and central to the dialectical viewpoint; all things without exception contain "internal contradictions" and it is this internal contradictoriness which is the "fundamental" cause of development in a thing or processes, while external relations between things are but secondary causes of development. "It is evident that purely external causes can only give rise to mechanical motion... but can...explain why things differ qualitatively in thousands of ways and why one thing changes into another" and that in the simple growth of plants and animals, for example, their quantitative development is chiefly the result of the internal contradictions. "Similarly, social development is due chiefly not to external but internal causes."

Since Mao has stated that the development of things and processes are triggered principally by internal causes, the "contradictoriness in things," with external causes a secondary factor, this generalization can then be applied to all phenomena. To stress that external factors are not responsible for development Mao stated that countries with almost the same geographical climate, an external factor, display great diversity and unevenness in their development. He further pointed out that great social changes can take place in one and the same country as in the case of the Russian revolution and China for which neither climate nor geography was responsible. The point Mao sought to make was that such changes were due principally to internal causes. "Changes in society are due chiefly to development of the internal contradictions in society, that is, the contradiction between the productive forces and the relations of production, the contradiction between classes and the contradiction between old and new . . . ."

According to Mao, it is the development of contradiction through struggle which advances society and gives the impetus for the suppression of the old society by the new. Thus, for a dialectician, no society is permanent, all will go out of existence to be replaced by new and different societal forms. It is the inevitability of the suppression of the old by the new which is the basis for the withering away of the communist party and the socialist state, and, in the futures, changes within the forms of communist society itself.

Although "internal causes" are the key to development, materialist dialectics do not exclude external causes. Materialist dialectics hold that external causes are the conditions of change and internal causes are the basis of change, and that external causes become operative through internal causes. Accordingly, a dialectical change has two separate but interrelated aspects; external and internal causes, or the conditions and basis of change respectively and without both internal and external causes development would be impossible. Mao illustrates this interrelatedness of internal and external causes, conditions and basis, by talking of an egg and a stone. "In a suitable temperature an egg changes into a chicken, but no temperature can change a stone into a chicken, because each has a different basis." At first glance this seems both a simple example and a statement of the obvious; hardly profound, and hardly the stuff with which to transform the world. As in the case of much of Mao's writing and with many of his examples it is precisely this sort of simplistically stated aphorism which has caused some to characterize Mao's writings and thought as of little consequence.

However, if we explore this statement we would find that it makes some interesting if not profound revolutionary points. For example, in an ideological and dialectical context it can be rephrased as follows: In a suitable temperature (external condition) an egg changes (internal cause or basis) into a chicken. In this case it is the external cause or condition which permits the internal cause to become operative and permits the egg to be transformed into a chicken. Clearly it is the internal development inside the egg which produces the chicken not the temperature. An explosive, for example, is a combination of ingredients which under certain conditions will produce an explosion. The condition or external cause which will produce the right conditions for an explosion is called "ignition" without which there can be no explosion.

In the same way it is the internal development inside a country which produces revolutionary activity and ultimately "a revolution," and not the external support of the Soviet Union, China, or the whole of the socialist camp. If the internal conditions do not favor a revolution it cannot happen; thus, communists cannot "export revolution" because the cause of revolution is internal and not external, though external conditions play an important role in helping the development of the internal causes when they do arise. The same ideal can also be applied to social development, war, revolution, and virtually all other aspects of man's activity. In a military example Mao stated that the external factors for two armies in battle may be essentially the same, geographic location, weather, terrain to some extent, and many other factors, yet, "In battle, one army is victorious and the other is defeated; both the victory and the defeat are determined by internal causes." One is victorious because it is strong and has competent leaders while the other is weaker with an incompetent leadership. It is through internal causes that external causes become operative. In citing a Chinese example Mao stated that the Soviet Union's October Socialist Revolution ushered in a new epoch in world history as well as in Russian history. Thus a revolution in Russia triggered by internal causes took place at a time when external conditions were favorable to its development, and in its success, their revolution became a favorable and helpful external cause or condition for revolutionary development in China and elsewhere. "It exerted influence on internal changes in other countries in the world and, similarly and in a particular profound way, on internal changes in China." In this fashion Mao acknowledged a debt to the "external causes" or "conditions for significant development" which are not derived solely from China's long history. Mao stated that the internal changes in China and other countries, though affected by the external causes, were still effected principally by inner laws, the internal development of the countries, "China included." In this fashion Mao showed the inter-action of external causes or conditions on the internal development taking place in other countries and without one there cannot be the other.

For Marxist-Leninists there are two opposing world outlooks which are locked in a permanent ideological struggle, between what they consider the old and backward outlook and the new and emerging outlook of the future. In every field of thought Marxist-Leninists counterpoise their views to those held by non-communists "against petty-bourgeoisie psychology - - new socialist psychology; against bourgeoisie individualism and indifference - - socialist collectivism and solidarity, against liberalism and patriarchal conservation - - our sound aggressive spirit; against personal ease and arrogance - - the spirit of sacrifice and action, modesty and demands upon oneself."

The work outlook of the Marxist-Leninists is of first importance to them. Without this revolutionary outlook there can be no world revolutionary movement. Communist parties continually stress the need to master Marxism-Leninism in a creative way and in so doing "fight scientifically against idealist and metaphysical concepts, and link our theory still more closely with revolutionary practice."

For Marxist-Leninists, ideology is used to fight against its enemies, and it is only through ideological struggle that their belief can be further developed.

The Albania Report states: Our theory can be developed and mastered only through struggle against its opponents. Opposing views and debate should be used in the party and the whole society. Any tendency towards conformism, to cover up contradictions, should be fought. Only in this way can we build up an active immunity to alien ideology. What are some of the practical results which stem from holding either of these contradictory points of view. In its essence, reality can be perceived in different ways depending upon the viewpoint and background of the observer. Thus a Satanist sees the world differently from a clergyman, an anarchist differently from a democrat, a barbarian differently from a civilized man, and as Mao points out, the dialectician sees reality differently from a "metaphysician," - - in an opposite way. This is particularly true of social phenomena.

One might disagree with the Communist point of view by stating that facts exist objectively and are incontrovertible. As such, they are common to all regardless of "outlook" and must be perceived by all in the same way. However logical this assertion may seem, a dialectician would disagree with it. A second question might then be asked, perhaps with some incredulity: "Is it possible that the same 'facts' could be so interpreted as to give a totally opposite point of view?" The answer is a resounding "Yes!" One of the clearer recent explanations of this apparent dichotomy was given by Chiang Han in a December 1973 *Peking Review* article entitled, "Great Benefits Derive from a Good Analysis." Chiang said: "From their varied class stands, people view and analyze problems from different points of departure and use different methods. This is why different and diametrically opposed conclusions may be reached on the same questions about the same material." Oleg Penkovsky in the book The Penkovsky Papers written in 1965 gave an example of the difference between the two points of view, and the results they produce when he described the problem of "outlook" between the dialectical thinkers of the Soviet Union and the non-dialectical thinkers of the non-Communist world. He stated that if someone were to hand an American general, a British general, and a Soviet general, "the same set of objective facts and scientific data, with instructions that these facts and data must be accepted as unimpeachable and an analysis made and conclusions drawn on the basis of them, the American and the Englishman might possibly reach the same conclusions - - I don't know. But the Soviet general would arrive at conclusions which would be radically different from the other two." Penkovsky then stated the reason for this is that the Soviet general begins with a totally different set of basic premises and preconceptions - - namely the Marxist view of history. "Secondary, the logical process of his mind is totally unlike that of his Western counterparts, because he uses Marxist dielectrics, whereas they will use some form of deductive reasoning."

Thus, if Marxist-Leninists believe that the dialectical view produces opposite conclusions, those which are "totally unlike" the conclusions developed by non-dialecticians, it is at least appropriate to ask the question of whether they then perceive their own reality and their own problems precisely as they are analyzed in the West, or if they see them differently - - partly differently - - or "totally unlike" the analyses produced in the West. For example, do the Communists perceive such concepts as détente and peaceful coexistence as a permanent "living together" or two "antagonistic social systems" or do they perceive "peaceful coexistence" as a form of struggle against imperialism and another way of fighting and defeating imperialism without resorting to a war which they could conceivably lose? Marxist-Leninists state over and over that the purpose of peaceful coexistence, and its leading aspect, détente, is to defeat the West without resorting to war. It is simply another and an efficient way to develop the revolutionary offensive all around the world.

When the Soviets speak of "Maosim" are they speaking of the Communist Party of China, and, conversely, when the Chinese speak of "Soviet revisionists" do they mean the Communist Party of the Soviet Union? The answer is that they do not, and neither party in the polemic has ever made an official statement to that effect. When the Socialist countries speak of non-alignment do they mean that countries should be neutral between the two camps? If so, they don't say so, but state that the principle condition of non-alignment is to be "anti-imperialist" and anti-colonialist". Against whom? We are told it is necessary to be non-aligned against the West, and principally the United States which they state supports imperialism and its puppets all around the world.

When the communists speak of "peace" do they mean simply the absence of war as it is so often conceived in the West, or do they mean something more and something else: It is clear that they mean the absence of war, but they also mean that this can only be accomplished by eliminating the basic cause of war and the social system it engenders and perpetuates it, namely capitalism. To achieve peace all "peace-loving" countries must attack the basic cause of wars, capitalism, eliminate it and in this way establish a world at peace. Thus, too, the permanent nature of the communist offensive as the leader of the "peace force" is to mobilize all the countries and the peoples of world under socialism to fight capitalism and develop socialism.

If these, and many, many other concepts are seen differently or in an "opposite" fashion by Marxist-Leninist dialecticians, then we must also ask if the Marxist-Leninist leaders and theoreticians understand the Sino-Soviet polemic in the same terms and in the same way as it is generally understood and interpreted by Western analysts. Or can it, as Mao states, be seen in quite an opposite way? Can the apparent irreconcilable division perceived by Western analysts be the predominate feature or relations between the Chinese and the Soviets, or can this very "division" be conducted in a special way, a dialectical way, and, in fact, be used to promote unity between China and the Soviet Union thus strengthening the entire socialist camp. Regardless of the point of view which one may hold the possibility must be admitted. It remains, therefore, to be seen if dialectical logic is sufficiently different to produce confusion in the minds of those who don't understand it and actually produce results which are contrary to those reached by formal and metaphysical logic.

Perhaps one more question should be asked at this point. Is the Marxist-Leninist dialectical method generally understood in either the Western or communist camp? The rhetorical answer is, of course, "No!" To understand the Marxist-Leninist dialectical method at the level at which it is presently developed and used by the most important communist parties in the world calls for long, persistent and arduous study of a great many highly ideological materials from the major parties of the communist movement as well as certain key works of Marx, Engels, Lenin and Mao Zedong. Even some of the leading figures in many communist parties are not proficient in dialectics, and Mao has criticized Stalin for his deficiencies in dialectics. A more recent statement by Mao highlights this view and was made while Mao was on a tour in August and September 1971. He stated in one of his talks that there should be much more study of the works of Marx, Engels and Lenin and added: "It just won't do if high-ranking cadres don't even know what is materialism and what is idealism." Perhaps the same thought might apply to high-level Western analysts!

World Revolutionary Strategy

By "The Insider"

The revolutionary struggle, which affects the fate of millions of people, calls for the same accurate planning as is needed, say, when launching a spaceship. Just as the conditions of space light are modeled beforehand in terms of mathematics, success in social planning depends on how thoroughly it is reasoned out with the help of materialist dialectics. Materialist dialectics is the methodological basis for the scientific interpretation and understanding of the social processes, for the correct determination of the political line in the most complex conditions and, at crucial moments, the guiding light in determining strategic aims and selecting tactics and forms and methods of the struggle.

- A. Sobelev: *World Marxist Review*, June 1964, "The Universality of Contradiction and the Concreteness of Truth," page 26.

An understanding of the dialectics of the universal and particular is of paramount importance if one is to grasp the essence of Marxist-Leninist revolutionary thought and action and the nature of the social revolution of the world proletariat. Marxist-Leninists see the revolution as a single worldwide process governed by common laws operating in different conditions.

121

As a consequence of geographic, social, cultural and national differences, the universal laws of the Marxist-Leninist world outlook manifest themselves differently from country to country. Lenin formulated the problem as follows:

> All nations will arrive at socialism - - this is inevitable, but all will do so in not exactly the same way, each will contribute something of its own to some form of democracy, to some variety of the dictatorship of the proletariat, to the varying rate of socialist transformations in the different aspects of social life.

There are then universal laws which govern the development of individual lives, societies, nations, revolution, in short, all objectively existing things. However, these universal and general laws become operative only in given concrete conditions, and as conditions vary from each other depending upon time and place, these general and universal laws will cause things and processes to develop differently within the framework of the concrete conditions existing at the point at which the laws are being applied. In consequence of this, the same revolutionary forms will manifest themselves differently in each country while still conforming to the general laws. For example, India and Thailand are both embarked upon a "national-democratic" revolution. India's conditions dictate that this revolutionary form be developed principally though not exclusively through parliamentary struggle while the conditions in

Thailand demand that the principle form of struggle be conducted principally through armed struggle with political and parliamentary struggle cosigned to a secondary but complimentary role.

It is because universal laws operate in different specific conditions that modern day socialism in China develops differently from the USSR. Both countries are developing socialism in accord with the universal materialist dialectical laws, but their development is neither equal nor identical simply because the conditions which exist for each are different. Each country must, therefore, constantly evaluate the conditions of their development so they may consistently apply the general revolutionary laws correctly. As they make mistakes they must reevaluate their work in order to see where they have misapplied the laws and then correct the mistakes. The course of the revolutionary process is complex and the dialectics of the universal and the particular must always be characterized by modifications, flexibility of forms, and, at the same time, by the stability of the essential laws and links which underlie all phenomena.

Marxist-Leninists believe their experience has shown that mankind's progress is governed by universal laws which they have identified and can apply to all things. Lenin said "the significant of the universal is contradictory: it is dead, impure, incomplete, etc., etc., but it alone is a stage towards knowledge of the concrete, for we can never know the concrete completely."

How does a Marxist-Leninist party seek to know the concrete and retain its orientation and general direction amidst innumerable diverse events and factors? Simply, it is the content of the socialist revolution following identified and proven universal laws of revolutionary transition from capitalism to socialism which enable them to relentlessly pursue their cause in spite of immense distractions and a multitude of conditions. However, the universal aspect of the laws of revolutionary development is not abstractly immutable, but are laws which deal with and apply to concrete and real events.

The universal nature of revolutionary development is in fact enriched through practice, through the real struggles of the world revolutionary forces to establish the socialist system universally throughout the world. Therefore, dialectics demands that the basic principles of revolutionary theory be applied and tested in a way "which will correctly modify these principles in certain particulars, correctly apply them to national and national-state distinctions. When Lenin speaks of modifying principles in particulars he is not, as it might seem, being opportunistic. What Lenin means is that which "is most essential is already encompassed in the universal and, consequently, is expressed in principles of theory."

To see the universal in its unity with which the particular is a distinctive feature of Marxist-Leninist methodology, and the two are inseparably linked and permanently interconnected and interpenetrating. A doctrinaire approach to general principles and laws would be to see the universal as a thing which is unchanging and self-contained dragged by philosophers from period to historical period always in the same form and with the same content. For a Marxist-Leninist; however, it is insufficient to know only the theoretical essence, but it must be perceived in its particular and concrete form at any given time. Soviet ideologue, Y. Krasin, in his book, *The Dialectics of Revolutionary Process,* outlined the principle criteria for determining the universal as follows:

> ...the universal has all the basic characteristics of an objective law: it expresses necessary and essential relations characterized by stability and recurrence.

Mao Zedong follows Lenin completely and states in his work, *On Contradiction*, that the basic law of dialectics, the universal law, is "The law of contradiction in things, that is, the law of the unity of opposites . . . This law, Mao states, "... exists in the process of development of all things...from beginning to end."

To understand the universality of contradiction and the law of the unity of opposites one must also deal with the particularity of contradiction since they are two aspects of the same thing. The universality of a thing, process or concept is directly derived from the particular aspects which are subsumed within or under the thing, process or concept.

Engels said, "The Marxist-Leninist view is that the law of materialistic dialectics, the law of the unity of opposites, is a universal law which governs nature, society and the development of thought, and which is applicable to the past, the present and the future. In other words, it is applicable to class society, to socialist society which is transitional between class and classless society, and also to the classless communist society of the future. Contradictions exist everywhere and at all times. They are differentiated into antagonistic and non-antagonistic contradictions. Contradictions are all irreconcilable and have to be solved through struggle. Contradictions and the struggles to resolve them are always the motive force that pushes human society forward."

He said, "The word is not to be regarded as a complex of ready-made things, but as a complex of processes, in which thing apparently stable, no less than their mind images in our heads, the concepts, go through an uninterrupted change of coming into being and passing away."

Thus, things are not seen as static or permanent, but as the result of a process within which things are developed and also degenerate. The "thing" per se is not basic but it is the process of "understanding change" which is fundamental. Therefore, a thing is something which comes into being and passes out of existence in a process of development. Cars and buildings are things which come into being through a process of development. Religion, atheism, revolution, the Sino-Soviet Polemic are also examples of "things" which have evolved in the process of development and which will eventually be eliminated in the process as it deepens and changes. All such things evolve as the result of inner development which comes into being when the external conditions are propitious for their existence and will pass away when the conditions change.

In discussing the universality of contradiction it is useful to understand what is meant by "contradiction" and through this explanation, the universal nature of the concept will become clearer. The non-dialectical definition is that a contradiction is a thing in opposition to another, or a condition in which things tend to be contrary. More specifically, and in non-dialectical terms, it means inconsistency and discrepancy, a condition in which two propositions are so related that if one is true the other is false. The tendency is to see contradiction occurring in ideals about things, but much less so in the things themselves.

Marxist-Leninists see contradiction in a different way and describe a dialectical contradiction as a "unity of opposites." By this they mean that all things contain contradiction each of which is composed of two and only two opposite aspects. They further state that each aspect is the condition for the other's existence. For example, war and peace are a unity of dialectical opposites, as are advance and retreat, socialism and capitalism, construction and destruction, virtue and sin, revisionism and orthodoxy, and so on. It is clear that in each such instance the one aspect is the condition for the existence of the other and without one there cannot be the other. There cannot, for example, be good without bad since the opposite of one or the other is the condition for understanding the total concept of good and evil. If one talks of the good he is also talking about bad even though the term may not be specifically mentioned. One cannot construct something without destroying something else, e.g., the communists cannot create and establish world socialism without destroying capitalism; nor can they create a communist world without destroying socialism. One cannot have a correct policy if there is not at the same time an incorrect policy. In this fashion such opposites are inseparably united, and, for a dialectician, he cannot consider one aspect without also taking the other into account. To fail to consider both in his work would be a betrayal of Marxism and Leninism, of the universal law of contradiction in things, the law of the unity of opposites, and would, in fact, be metaphysical.

There is still another side of this law of the unity of opposites which is implicit in it, i.e., if there is a unity of opposites there must also exist its dialectical opposite, the "struggle of opposites," and it is precisely the unity of the two opposites which makes conflict between them inevitable. When viewed with a certain perspective one might also say it is a matter of common sense. After all, history is replete with examples of a continual conflict between the forces of war and peace, of struggle between classes such as the slaves and slave owners, the proletariat and the bourgeoisie; of a conflict between a socialist and a capitalist system, and many, many other examples could be cited. Thus, dialectically a thing or process contains both unity and division at the same time. It is simply a matter of "viewpoint" or "outlook", a way to look at and analyze reality. The fact that some may choose to use still other viewpoints which they consider equally valid in no way diminishes the Marxist-Leninist dialectical world outlook, nor its value and unity to their interpretation of reality and its application to the development of the world revolutionary struggle.

Opposites united in a contradiction struggle against and seek domination over the other through their mutual interpenetration. Since the opposites are united in a permanent struggle, each opposite at any given moment of the struggle is partially penetrated by the other thus influencing and modifying the other aspect in diverse ways and each of the two aspects is constantly affected by the nature of its relationship to the other. In dealing with this Mao formulated the law of the unity and struggle of opposites into an expression commonly and frequently stated as "one divides into two," and which succinctly summarizes the essence of the dialectical method.

Chairman Mao pointed out: "Everything divides into two." "In Society as in nature, every entity invariably breaks up into its different parts, only there are differences in content and form under different concrete conditions." Chairman Mao's brilliant thesis that one divides into two is a penetrating and concise generalization of the law of the unity of opposites; it is a great development of materialist dialectics.

Since "everything divides into two" Mao states that the universality or absoluteness of contradiction has a "twofold" meaning. "One is that contradictions exist in the process of development of all things, and the other is that in the process of development of each thing a movement (struggle) of opposites exists from beginning to end." In this Mao remains faithful to Engels and Lenin who had expressed themselves on the subject in the same way. Mao further stated, "The interdependence (unity) of the contradictory aspects present in all things and the struggle between these aspects determine the life (development) of all things and push their development forward. There is nothing which does not contain contradiction; without contradiction nothing would exist."

In applying these ideals to some practical examples one can reach some interesting conclusions about the way in which a dialectician sees reality - - his reality. That there are contradictions between the two opposite and opposing social systems, capitalism and socialism, is readily apparent to anyone familiar with current events. That such contradictions are a normal and natural consequence of the dialectical world outlook is in conformance with the universal law of the unity and struggle of opposites as perceived by Marxist-Leninists whether or not non-Marxists agree or disagree. However just as there are contradictions

130

between the two opposing social systems, as well as among the countries which compose them, so to, according to the universal nature of contradiction, must there be contradictions between and among the socialist countries, and between and among the communist parties which control them. Since contradictions are contained in all things and are irreconcilable, so to are the contradictions which exist between and among communist parties. Since the dialectical methodology dictates that contradictions must be resolved through struggle, the differences which exist, and must exist, between the Chinese and Soviets for example, must also be resolved through struggle, just as the victory of either the capitalist or socialist system will be decided by the irreconcilable struggle between the two systems.

Thus, the Sino-Soviet polemic is a logical and natural consequence of the Marxist-Leninist ideology and outlook. It would be insufficient, however, to leave the idea at this point since it might well create some difficulties for the reader later on. Therefore, it should be mentioned here, and discussed in detail in later pages, that contradiction itself, like everything else, can be divided into "two kinds of contradiction of a different nature," antagonistic and non-antagonistic contradictions. In the case of the antagonistic contradiction between the "people" and their enemies, capitalism and socialism, all forms of struggle must be used to resolve these irreconcilable contradictions, both violent and non-violent. In the case of non-antagonistic contradictions which exist among the Communist parties, the "people," those who share common interests and goals even though they may differ about how to accomplish them at times, the form of struggle to resolve these irreconcilable contradictions is criticism and self-criticism. Thus the Sino-Soviet polemic, for example, is a form of mutual criticism employed by the Chinese and Soviets to resolve contradictions among themselves and within the movement and to educate all other Marxist-Leninist through this open debate. Thus the Sino-Soviet polemic is in conformance with the ideological principles.

This view was further confirmed in a *People's Daily and Red Flag* editorial published on February 4, 1964, which was subsequently incorporated in the book, *The Polemic On the General Line of the International Communist Movement*, printed in Peking in 1965, in which the purpose of the Sino-Soviet polemic were made quite clear:

> . . . only through public debate, setting forth the facts and reasoning things out will it be possible to clarify matters, distinguish right from wrong and safeguard and strengthen the unity of the internal communist movement on the basis of Marxism-Leninism and proletarian internationalism.
>
> Marxism-Leninism is a science, and science fears no debate. Anything which fears debate is no science. The present great debate in the international communist movement is impelling Communists, revolutionists and

revolutionary people in all countries to use their brains and ponder over problems concerning the revolution in their own countries and the world revolution in accordance with the fundamental theories of Marxism-Leninism. Through this great debate, people will be able to distinguish between right and wrong and between real and sham Marxism-Leninism. Through this great debate all the revolutionary forces in the world will be mobilized and all Marxist-Leninist will be tempered ideologically and politically and will be able to integrate Marxism-Leninism with concrete practice in their own countries in a more mature way. Thus Marxism-Leninism will undoubtedly further enrich, developed and raised to new heights.

Thus, while the particular character of the "great debate" will be carried out principally between China and the Soviet Union it simultaneously has a "universal" aspect which transcends the differences between the two participants. The universal nature of the polemic is the benefit derived through the development and enrichment of the science of Marxism-Leninism and the educative value it holds for Marxist-Leninists everywhere, and the entire strengthening of the entire communist movement which results.

By way of further explanation of the "universality of contradiction" Engels said, ". . . life consists precisely and primarily in this - - that a being is at each moment itself and at the same time something else runs directly opposite to many who hold the view that a thing is what it is and nothing else - - it is either this thing or some other thing but not both itself and something else. For example, an airplane is an airplane and cannot at the same time be something else. The outlook of non-dialecticians tells them that if a person has life he does not possess non-life; A is A and it cannot be non-A; things are either-or, but not both. The dialectical approach, however, says "that a being is at each moment itself and yet something else." This approach to reality pervades all aspects of dialectical methodology. In conformance with the basic principle of dividing things into two opposites, questions are also divided into two kinds; there are dialectical and non-dialectical questions, and the answers are similarly divided. For a Marxist-Leninist dialectician a non-dialectical question is one which refers to things in which no development takes place, and these are also divided into two, metaphysical and academic questions.

Metaphysical questions correspond to purely "subjective" questions which Marxist-Leninists do not regard as Marxist truths, and the answers to all such questions are "no." For example, if one asks, ""Does God exist?" "Is Christ the son of God?" "Is the bible the word of God?" "Did God create the universe?" The answer is always, "no." An academic question, on the other hand, always refers to a matter of "objective fact" and a Marxist-Leninist will answer either "yes" or "no" depending upon the nature of the questions. To the question "Is Moscow the capital of China?", the answer is, "no", while to a question such as asking if Beethoven was a European composer of classical music the answer would be "yes."

On the other hand, the dialectical question is always related to a process of development of a thing - - something which has a beginning, goes through a process of development and change, and has an end. This too can be "divided into two," has two meanings, and is never answered "yes" or "no." A dialectical question is concerned with the development of a thing from the present to the future or is exclusively directed to the current situation. If the question concerns the current situation the reply will be "the two -- both/all." For example, if the question were asked: "Which of Mao's essays, *On Contradiction* or *On Practice* is the more important?" The answer is not either one or the other, but "both depending upon the conditions." This is a matter of common sense, of course, and in this case the "conditions" for determining which is more important than the other depends upon the purpose of the study, what one wants to learn. In another instance, if the questions were asked: "Of all Mao's writings which is the most important?: Again, it would be inappropriate to give a categorical answer, either a "yes" or a "no." The dialectical answer would be "all are important - - it depends upon the conditions." What conditions? Those which direct the study, and explain what one seeks to learn at the time of the study.

In a process which is concerned with the development of a thing from the present to the future the answer is always "yes" and "no" at the same time, or as Mao has sometimes phrased it, "yes it is and yet it is not." One might ask how it can be both good and bad for the movement at the same time, to which the dialectician would answer, "It depends upon the conditions." In certain conditions the polemic is a good thing because the essence of the polemic is incorrectly understood by Western analysts thus resulting in their development of incorrect analysis and policies based upon their misconceptions. At the same time it is a bad thing because it simultaneously but temporarily misleads many Marxist-Leninists without a deep knowledge of dialectics. Many similar double responses can be developed to the same question but the point is that the Sino-Soviet polemic has both negative and positive features for both the non-communist and the communist camp, and the double dialectical response is the only one which can readily develop the true conditions of the Sino-Soviet polemic. The ramifications of this double response are too complex to detail in this chapter, but will become clearer in future chapters. This dialectical response, based on Engel's thought that a thing is itself and at the same time something else, is a logical consequence of the dialectical approach and the doctrinal basis for it is shared by all Marxist-Leninists.

In his essay, *On Practice*, Mao provides a clear example of this dialectical response when he talks of the interrelatedness of theory and practice and asks a question concerning it: "When we get to this point, is the movement of knowledge completed? Our answer is: it is and yet it is not." In his essay, "Talks at the Yenan Forum on Culture and Art," Mao is talking about the failure of some artists to understand the correct position towards the production of literary and art work, and says it is a matter of "attitude." "From one's stand there follow specific attitudes towards specific matters. For instance, is one to extol or expose? This is a question of attitude. Which attitude is wanted? I would say both. The question is, whom are you dealing with?"

This method of reasoning is universal among top-level Marxist-Leninists and even though Communists may seem only to talk of one side of an issue the dialectical implicitness of the double response is always there. Some other examples should help further illustrate this important point. Are the communists for war? Since war is a process of development, contains a beginning and ending, this can be considered a dialectical question and the correct answer is "yes, the communists are for war, and yet they are not." How, can the communists be both for and against war? To answer this question let us add one other dialectical principle; "it depends upon the conditions." Thus, "under certain conditions" the communists are for war and other and different conditions they are not. Therefore, if we use the same dialectical division of "war" which the communists make, if we divide war into two, we find that there are two kinds of war, just and unjust. Just and unjust wars are dialectical opposites, and the "conditions" determine the kind of war which they are "for" and "against." It is apparent, since they are doing the defining, that a "just war" is a revolutionary war conducted by a people, a country, or nation, against imperialism or their enemies of the world revolutionary process. Thus, the communists are "for" this war since in the given "conditions" it is favorable to their side. At the same time communists oppose "unjust" wars. Unjust wars are those which are carried out by non-revolutionary or counter-revolutionary forces which, in their essence, are directed against the world's revolutionary forces and serve the interests of capitalists, fascists, social democrats, the bourgeoisie, any race, group, or country which opposes the world socialist revolution. They are against these "unjust" wars.

Are the communists for revolution? One can presume that if that question were asked of most metaphysical thinkers the immediate response would be a quick and unequivocal "yes." Yet the answer is that the communists are "for revolution, and yet they are not." They are for socialist revolutions which develop the world revolutionary struggle, while they oppose a revolution, for example, which would seek to overthrow a socialist government, or a government of a country which they regard as "progressive" and in support of general communist objectives against capitalism and imperialism. To give an idea of another dialectical answer a question might be asked like this: "Are the communists for revisionism or orthodoxy." Here the answer would be, "they are for both. It depends upon the conditions." It is easy to see the conditions necessary for orthodoxy and to understand them, but much more obscure are the reasons or conditions they are also for revisionism. What are these conditions? The communists are "for" revisionism as a negative example to fight "against" in order to better promote their communist orthodoxy. The communists are "for" revisionism when it is used as a subterfuge to fool the enemy who does not understand the role of revisionism in promoting the socialist factors in society. The communists are "for" revisionism when it is used as an educational tool for the strengthening of the socialist society, etc.

For Communists, contradiction, the unity of two opposites in thing or process locked in irreconcilable struggle, is present in the development of all things. Contradiction permeates the process of development from beginning to end - - this is the universality of contradiction, and there is nothing in the world which does not contain contradiction.

We may now say a few words to sum up. The law of contradiction in things, that is the law of the unity of opposites, is the fundamental law of nature and society and therefore also the fundamental law of thought. It stands opposed to the metaphysical world outlook. It represents a revolution in the history of human knowledge. According to dialectical materialism, contradictions are present in all processes of objectively existing things and of subjective thought and permeates all these processes from beginning to end; this is the universality and absoluteness of contradiction.

The practical struggle which they wage on all fronts will ultimately determine the victor. The internal struggle among and between communists, e.g., the Chinese and Soviets, is an integral part of the same struggle and is a manifestation of the "universality of contradiction." There must be differences among communists if development of the world communist system is to take place. In contrast to the antagonistic differences which exist between the two social systems, the contradictions between or among communists are of a non-antagonistic nature and must be resolved on the basis of Marxist-Leninist principle using the method of criticism and self-criticism, itself a form of struggle. Whereas in the case of the conflict between socialism and capitalism the former seeks the destruction of the latter, the same cannot be said of the dispute between the Chinese and the Soviets. There is no official statement in the literature of either party or government that it seeks the destruction of the other. Rather, the criticism each levies against the other is pleaful admonition to get back onto the orthodox Marxist-Leninist path from which each seems to believe the other has strayed.

Communist Parties in the World

The official list of parties at the 15th International Meeting of Communist and Workers Parties (IMCWP), held November 2013, in Lisbon, Portugal:

- Algerian Party For Democracy and Socialism
- Communist Party of Argentina
- Communist Party of Australia
- Communist Party of Azerbaijan
- Bahrain, Democratic Progressive Tribune
- Communist Party of Belarus
- Workers' Party of Belgium
- Brazilian Communist Party
- Communist Party of Brazil
- Communist Party of Britain
- Communist Party of Bulgaria
- Communist Party of Canada
- Communist Party of Chile
- Communist Party of China
- Colombian Communist Party
- Communist Party of Cuba
- Progressive Party of The Working People – AKEL (Cyprus).
- Communist Party of Bohemia And Moravia
- Communist Party In Denmark
- Communist Party of Denmark
- Communist Party of Egypt
- Communist Party of Ecuador
- Communist Party of Finland
- French Communist Party
- Unified Communist Party of Georgia

- German Communist Party
- Communist Party of Greece
- Guadalupean Communist Party
- People's Progressive Party, Guyana
- Hungarian Workers' Party
- Communist Party of India
- Communist Party of India (Marxist)
- Tudeh Party of Iran
- Iraqi Communist Party
- Communist Party of Ireland
- The Workers' Party of Ireland
- Communist Party of Israel
- Party of The Italian Communists
- Workers' Party of Korea
- Laos, Peoples' Revolutionary Party
- Socialist Party of Latvia
- Lebanese Communist Party
- Communist Party of Luxembourg
- Communist Party of Malta
- Communist Party of Mexico
- Party of Communists of Rep. of Moldova
- New Communist Party of The Netherlands
- Communist Party of Norway
- Communist Party of Pakistan
- Palestinian Communist Party
- Palestinian People's Party
- Panama, Party of The People
- Peruvian Communist Party
- Communist Party of Poland
- Portuguese Communist Party
- Romania, Socialist Alliance Party

- Communist Party of Russian Federation
- Communist Workers Party of Russia (RKRP)
- Russia, Union of Communist Parties
- Russia, Communist Party of Soviet Union
- New Communist Party of Yugoslavia
- South African Communist Party
- Communist Party of Spain
- Communist Party of The People of Spain
- Party of Communists of Cataluna
- Communist Party of Sri-lanka
- Sudanese Communist Party
- Syrian Communist Party
- Communist Party of Tadjikistan
- Communist Party of Turkey (TKP)
- Labour Party (EMEP), Turkey
- Communist Party of Ukraine
- Union of Communists of Ukraine
- Communist Party of Uruguay
- Communist Party USA

End Notes

---

[1] http://www.nkfreedom.org/

[2] Blaine Harden, "Can we believe all the horrors described by North Korean escapees?," The Washington Post, August 9, 2015.

[3] http://www.portal-credo.ru/site/?act=english&id=281

[4] http://nationalinterest.org/blog/the-buzz/russia-hold-joint-military-drills-north-korea-cuba-12178

[5] *Global Taxes for World Government* is available at www.noglobaltaxes.org *Global Bondage* is out of print but the text has been posted at https://archive.org/stream/GlobalBondage/Global-Bondage-The-United-Nations-Plan-To-Rule-The-World-by-Cliff-Kincaid_djvu.txt

[6] http://americamagazine.org/issue/call-virtue

[7] Russia's role in world revolution also figures prominently in the Fatima revelations about Russia becoming a source of errors throughout the world. The Catholic view is that the Virgin Mary appeared to the children at Fatima, Portugal, in 1917 and requested the consecration of Russia, and the controversy is whether the consecration did occur.

[8] See Ginni Thomas interview at http://dailycaller.com/2015/07/29/expert-america-doing-next-to-nothing-about-chinas-growing-power/

[9] Hay favored adult-child sex, the next phase in the dialectic of sexual rights that is even now a subject of conversation, debate, and discussion.

[10] Elizabeth Yore, an attorney and international child rights advocate, served as one of the members of the Heartland Institute delegation to protest the Vatican exclusion of all scientific opinions and reliance on population control experts for the encyclical.

[11] Green Cross International says it "enjoys consultative status with the United Nations Economic and Social Council, and United Nations Educational, Scientific and Cultural Organization." Further, it is an admitted observer organization with the United Nations Framework Convention on Climate Change.

[12] Gussack's books include *Sowing the Seeds of Our*

Destruction: Useful Idiots on the "Right."

[13] Marx, Karl. "On the Question of Free Trade," February 1848 Accessed From:
http://www.marxists.org/archive/marx/works/1848/01/09ft.htm

[14] http://farc-epeace.org/index.php/general-information-farc-ep.html

[15] "Putin Threatens America with Nuclear Annihilation," http://www.aim.org/aim-column/putin-threatens-america-with-nuclear-annihilation/

[16] The ASI website, www.religiousleftexposed.com, examines the leftward drift of the Roman Catholic Church

[17] *The Communist: Frank Marshall Davis - The Untold Story of Barack Obama's Mentor.*

[18] Markovsky wrote the book, *Anatomy of a Bolshevik: How Marx & Lenin Explain Obama's Grand Plan.*

[19] *Forcing Change* newsletter, Volume 9, Issue 6. Also see www.debrarae.us

[20] America's Survival, Inc. held a news conference to rebut Fox News personality Megyn Kelly for a "Kelly File" interview of Obama associate and terrorist Bill Ayers, which amounted to his rehabilitation. We informed Fox News CEO Roger Ailes that Kelly was poorly prepared for this interview and she created a false narrative and impression of the activities of Ayers and his communist killer comrades.

[21] See http://canisiusbooks.com/articles/feminism_russian-weapon-against-family.htm

[22] See http://www.usasurvival.org/home/docs/abzug1.pdf

[23] Their book is titled, *Reagan at Westminster: Foreshadowing the End of the Cold War.*

[24] During a Vatican visit, stopped to cross himself and kiss an icon of the Madonna that he gave to Pope Francis.

[25] See "Why Is the Vatican Pushing Communist Goals?" at http://www.lepantoinstitute.org/sustainable-development-goals/vatican-pushing-communist-goals/

[26] http://www.unoamerica.org

[27] See www.TrevorLoudon.com

[28] When I once questioned Hartmann about how much the Russians were paying him, he actually grabbed my camera recording his response in order to avoid being seen stonewalling.

[29] *The Red-Green Axis: Refugees, Immigration and the Agenda to Erase America.*

[30] http://www.familysecuritymatters.org/publications/detail/who-is-is

[31] Merkel, who grew up in the formerly communist East Germany and spent 35 years of her life under the dictatorship, is the subject of a book by Günther Lachmann and Ralf Georg Reuth titled, *The First Life of Angela M.,* which suggests that she had deeper ties to the communist regime than previously known or acknowledged

45483277R00084

Made in the USA
Charleston, SC
23 August 2015